Anthony

BOOKS BY

THEODORE H. WHITE

CAESAR
AT THE
RUBICON

CAESAR
AT THE
RUBICON

A PLAY ABOUT POLITICS

THEODORE H.^{arold} WHITE

ATHENEUM

NEW YORK

1968

Copyright © 1968 by Theodore H. White
All rights reserved
Library of Congress catalog card number 67-25479
Published simultaneously in Canada by McClelland and Stewart Ltd.
Manufactured in the United States of America by H. Wolff, New York
Designed by Harry Ford
First Edition

For David K. E. Bruce

AUTHOR'S NOTE

I WOULD like to say my thanks to all who helped make this book possible:

Most importantly I owe thanks to the Rockefeller Foundation, whose hospitality made the Villa Serbelloni, close by Caesar's Novum Comum, my shelter while writing the dramatic action of this story. I owe my gratitude to the Institute for Classical Studies of London University for letting me use their magnificent library. I owe further thanks to the Frederick Lewis Allen Room of the New York Public Library and the Classical Library of Harvard University for help in research.

A number of scholars have been particularly helpful with their time and guidance, particularly: Professors Lily Ross Taylor of Bryn Mawr; J. P. V. D. Balsdon of Oxford; Mason Hammond of Harvard; Ernst Badian of the University of Leeds; Thomas Wilson of the Harvard University Press; and too many others to name. No one, however, is responsible for the errors, fancies, hypotheses and aberrations of this manuscript except myself.

To Mrs. Shirley Farmer Kessel I owe belated thanks for her devoted original research on this project.

CONTENTS

CAESAR
AT THE
RUBICON

PROLOGUE

W HO HE WAS, or what he was, or what manner of man he was—no one knows for sure. Every age has carved its own Caesar, dressing him with its own passions and fears, tonguing him with the wit and wisdom of its passing moment. So we know of Caesar the tyrant and Caesar the merciful; of Caesar the killer and Caesar the lawmaker; of Caesar the wise and Caesar the lover; and of Caesar the Deified.

Two episodes of ripping violence have gripped the imagination of all men who have tried to recall Caesar—the Act at the Rubicon and the Act of Assassination. But old history makes both these acts too simple. Caesar was so big, he has been seen generally only in outline. Before his time the world of Rome was set in one direction, and because of him that world turned about. No other single individual—except the Christ—caused so great a change in Western man's thinking. Legends sprang from him; he had a power, a force, a genius that crowded everything but his personality out of the thinking of Rome in his own time and for centuries thereafter.

Yet, beneath all legends was a man: born Gaius Julius Caesar, probably in 102 B.C. And I, in this study, have been trying to explore not what history says he did, but how he may have felt while doing it. Of this complicated man we know much that we have for millennia either misunderstood or been trying to forget; but today, as history swings through an echoing cycle, he appears once again fresh—perhaps more a man of our time than of any other time but his own.

Barbarian, primitive, savage though Caesar's Rome may have been, men tormented themselves and each other in that city and time with the same problems of freedom, of law, of order, of discipline, of empire that torment us today. Mobs rioted in Rome's streets in a tempo of ferocity that surpassed by far the civil violence of our time. Wars on distant frontiers lured the legions on and on to adventures no stay-at-home could comprehend. Romans indulged themselves, in Caesar's time, with the same carnal pleasures of flesh, of drink, of revel that lately have become our way of life, too.

A pagan cruelty totally alien to us was, however, commonplace. Death and killing in public places was a matter of games and entertainment; murder was political tactic; and extermination was foreign policy. The great historic challenge to man's casual inhumanity was not to come for another two generations when the Christ spoke for mercy; but already, in Caesar, one finds a first serious questioning of the limits of force; for he, who understood killing better than any other man of his time, came to recognize that force and cruelty alone could not create the order which he sought; thus, in him one sees the first tentative exploration of mercy as a policy of government. If, in the end, in his barbarian world, he reached the limit of reason and stepped across the borderline to madness— this, too, is not unfamiliar in our age of paranoiac dictators.

The problem in writing of Caesar is that he was, at once, so naturally barbarian—and so thoroughly, relevantly, modern, too. The facts can be read either way.

There are, to be sure, fragments of fact on which all scholars, romantics, mythmakers do agree:

The man himself, of course: tall, gaunt, thin of lip, long of neck (with ugly, wrinkled neck folds), pale of skin, black of eyes, balding. Handsome he must have been as a youth. But we can see him only in profile in the coins he approved as self-portraits at the end of his days as Dictator—the unflattering image of an ugly, yet attractive, rogue, the faintest trace of some sardonic smile on his lips.

Much more vivid is the outline he draws of himself in his writing: the silhouette of the horseman in scarlet cape, the cape flaring back against the wind, the horse always galloping. Through the writing surges always a furious impatience—a slow, calculated waiting, and then the controlled speed of his action when it bursts. What remains to us of his writings is almost entirely of war, and thus the pace of his action is exaggerated. He chooses clear targets, then instantly strikes, his men moving at forced march by day and night, faster than any other troops of antiquity, advancing at the dog-trot, opening combat always on the dash.

Yet over and over again, in these writings, these stark accountings of action, his rhythm breaks, and there come those characteristic Caesarian passages of curiosity and wonderment. He crosses the Channel to scourge the savage Britons—and diverts himself and the reader with reflection on the mystery of the Druids; again, diverts attention to a mechanical examination of how men build coracles of skin; suspends his bloody story of the

Gallic conquest to entertain himself and Romans with an anthropologist's study of the customs of the Gauls; halts the flow of action to invite the reader with a description of the flow of a river; and, again and again, pauses in storytelling to muse on panic, courage, leadership, infection of rumor, as men clash with men in stress.

It is in these strange, subordinate reflections that one has the most authentic echo of the Caesar of politics—the furious, perplexed, yet thoughtful man who mystified a generation that could not even dimly guess his ultimate purpose.

For he *was* a mystery to his time.

Romans had watched him grow: offspring of a once-great patrician family, now decayed; orphaned in a time of trouble; and pledged by the doting women who brought him up to be a priest—a *flamen dialis* (had he become a *flamen dialis*, the world would never have known history's Caesar; those servants of Jupiter's Temple were forbidden to gaze upon a dead body, view an army in array of war, mount a horse or spend more than a day away from Rome). Politics prevented his induction as a temple priest, and so he graduated, a teen-ager, to the education normal for a boy of his time—tactics of war and rhetoric for the Forum. He dabbled in poetry as a youth (later, when he became Dictator, it is said that he caused all his poetry to be burned, a mark of editorial good taste that few other dictators have even fleetingly considered), then became a fashionable young man with a gift for politics. As a politician he was a "traitor to his class," the nobility—for he was of the party of "*populares*," those who claimed to speak for the masses and learned to organize their votes. As a politician-organizer, he became a master, climbing steadily through elective offices up the ladder of honors—quaestor, aedile, praetor, consul; briber, grafter, vote manipulator, boss, speech-maker. A sportsman of the bed (after the death of his first wife), he apparently couched with every Roman matron he could reach, specializing in the wives and sisters of enemies, friends and partners (old rumor has it that he seduced the wives of both partners in his first triumvirate); tasted the women, young and old, of every age and country; kept a stable of gladiators as men now keep a stable of horses—but beyond that an ascetic who rarely drank and had no particular craving for fine food.

Romans watched his early career, not quite under-standing—he fostered a law to let the High Priesthood (Pontifex Maximus) be chosen by popular vote, and then got himself elected. Engineered deals, politics, arrange-ments for older, more stupid men until in 59 B.C. he him-self emerged at the political summit as consul. Where-upon he threw all Rome into turmoil with his laws and reforms.

Thus, Rome was glad to be rid of him when he asked, out of what ambition his enemies could not fathom, that he be given command of the bloody northern front, the war against the Gauls and Germans.

And when, after nine years, he came back from that war, there was no Gaul any longer and the Germans cowered in fright. But the Caesar who came back was even more mysterious than the one who had left.

For, as in any great man, there were many Caesars.

The Caesar who came back was the Dictator-to-be, and this was the Caesar they killed on the Ides of March, 44 B.C. This Caesar, the Dictator, is the man who cramps our memories still. There is the echo of this Caesar in all that we do today; in our calendar, which counts twelve months, beginning in January, reaching midsummer in July (named for himself) as he ordained it; this is the Caesar whose name is an epithet or adjective of common use in every language of the Western world; this is the Caesar whose name or title cloaked every Kaiser, Tsar, Imperator or Emperor who has aspired to world dominion since.

Of this Caesar—his laws, his victories, his decrees, his sunset affair with Cleopatra, his death—we have been told over and over again since men began to write history. It is this Caesar who has fascinated almost as many great writers as the Christ himself; yet all have seen him at the end of life. Shakespeare, drawing him from Plutarch, made him the moody tyrant, creature of fate. Shaw made him the witty, detached adventurer, toying with life and empire as a game; Mommsen made him the brooding genius, shaper of the future. In our time, Thornton Wilder has made him the urbane and cynical phrasemaker, world-weary, soul-tired, helplessly awaiting his end, yet amused as the end approaches.

But there was another earlier Caesar, a Caesar all too often forgotten and far more kin to us than to the people of his time.

This other Caesar was oddly modern and romantic. A youth of eighteen, married to the young Cornelia whom he loved, ordered by Sulla, the cruelest Dictator of the age, to divorce her—this Caesar refused to divorce his wife, and fled with her to the hills because he loved her. (While Pompey, later his great rival, then a young man, too, divorced his pregnant wife because the Dictator told him to do so.) This early Caesar was the man who all alone in the Roman Senate stood to insist that the co-conspirators of Catiline be given fair and open trial as the law required before being put to death; and risked his life to make the point that all free men must have fair trial before the passage of judgment. This was the Caesar who (some scholars insist) shocked every decent senator by inventing the world's first newspaper— the Acta Diurna, posted on the walls of Rome during his first consulate, an open account of the proceedings (hitherto secret) of the Senate so that the people might read and know the talk and debate of their leaders.

Above all, this early Caesar was a man of politics. Rome was a Republic; the people were sovereign; their votes made power. To sway those votes was to sway power itself, and thus he invented, or developed, many of those techniques and devices so familiar to us in our manipulation of popular votes today. This horrified his aristocratic colleagues, who expected to decide among themselves who should lead, and than receive from the people simple, uncomplicated assent to what they proposed. Caesar changed all this, for, as a *"popularis,"* a man of the people's party, he taught the people all too well how great was their power and turned them against what he called the *"factio paucorum,"* the "clique of the few," the Establishment of the day.

Between the two Caesars, the early Caesar of the *populares* and the later Caesar, Dictator, a transformation of personality so great intervenes that it cries for understanding. This exercise in melodrama is an attempt to catch the episode of transformation.

The name of the episode is the Rubicon.
Every schoolboy in the Western world knows that

Caesar crossed the Rubicon—even though no one today can distinguish which of the three little gullies that fall off the shoulder of Sant' Arcangelo, just north of Rimini, is actually Caesar's Rubicon.

The Rubicon is more than an event, more even than a watershed. It was tragedy, one of the half-dozen great tragedies of human civilization. With the crossing of the Rubicon in 49 B.C., five hundred years of experiment in self-government failed.

Only a century before, Polybius, the Greek historian, had described Rome to the world as the supreme triumph of republican achievement, the solid proof that not only could citizens rule themselves, but that no other way of government had ever been more successful. Each year the people elected two leaders, twin consuls, to direct the state. An august Senate, its members all former magistrates elected over the years by the people, consulted with each other and the consuls, who then offered proposals of new law to the citizens. Once the citizens, assembled in voting files, had approved these laws, the whole became one: SPQR—*Senatus Populusque Romanus*—the Roman state united in arms and faith to challenge all. Judges and juries meted out even-handed justice to all who held citizenship and "*fiat justitia, ruat coelum*" ("let justice be done though the heavens fall"). The Senate approved treaties, proposed commands and generals; and once the people in Assembly approved, armies marched forth and the world trembled.

Polybius wrote only a generation before it all began to dissolve, at the apogee of the Republic, with Carthage and Greece both defeated. Roman women in those days spun wool, educated their children, shunned games, theaters and public appearances; ceremonies were observed;

distinguished citizens worked their own fields; it was an honor to serve as soldier, and only property-owning citizens qualified to bear arms. But the very success of the Republic undermined it. Even as Polybius wrote, wealth of conquest was pouring in; mobs in the street were soon demanding their share; leaders and senators grew rich; generals began to sense the power of their arms and raise their own troops; amusement, luxury and fornication changed the image of the Roman woman from Cornelia, mother of the Gracchi, to Clodia, the aristocratic harlot of the Tiber.

All this had been happening for sixty years (from the time of the Gracchi) before Caesar left for Gaul as a political soldier. In Rome there were only two noble occupations—war and politics; but an accelerating squalor and greed divorced them from the older self-lessness and patriotism of which Polybius wrote. Caesar went north, snatching his combat command as political spoils, his authority won from the Assembly and Senate, as British guards officers once won their commission, by favor in high place and ready cash on the table.

The man who left Rome was seen by the Roman establishment and its world of fashion as a deft and subtle politician, a master of words, rhetoric and demagoguery. But little more than that. In gossip he was—as Catullus, that marvelous poet, describes him—the "white cock-pigeon" bouncing through every bed of Rome. Of him, the most they could hope for was that he might guard the Alpine passes; and many hoped that in those Alpine passes or on their gloomy western slopes he would lose his life.

* * *

The military problem before him was the problem that had haunted Romans for four hundred years: the barbarians beyond the Alpine wall. For centuries, Gauls and Germans had come raiding, wheeling, killing, howling up to the foothills of the passes to harass and burn the frontier, to threaten the great Po valley, the fairest land in all Italy.

To this problem Caesar brought not only new tactics —his triple-line formation, his new-type javelin, novel engineering and logistic inventions—but also his élan and ability to inspire infantry.

All these he used in a simple strategy: His enemy were tribesmen who fought by no accepted rules in what, today, we might call total guerrilla war. There is only one way to crush guerrilla warfare—it is to go for the cities, the homes, the shelters. It is to kill women, children, old people, innocents, all alike, as one forces the enemy to protect his dear ones. You erase the base in which irregular warfare breeds, you purge it. Caesar purged Gaul. In nine years he branded it, seared it, scorched it.

The dark and gloomy cliffs of the Alps were transformed by Caesar from a military barrier to a simple geographical feature on Europe's wrinkled surface. He crossed the Rhine and struck terror into the Germans; he crossed the Channel and bloodied the Britons. When he was through with his work, the barbarian wars were over—in Gaul forever, in Germany for generations. And all done by a handful of foot-soldiers—never more than fifty thousand men to put an end to the civilization of fifteen million Gauls. At any moment, all might have been lost; a single misjudgment, a single siege gone wrong, a single rashness, and he would have been swallowed by the forests and by history.

Yet he was not. He triumphed.

The man who returned, thus, after nine years of war in Gaul at the end of 50 B.C. to claim triumphal honors, as was the ancient custom, was entirely different from the master politician who had left, the ladies'-man of gossip. The man returning was Caesar Imperator.

To both sides it must have seemed absurd.

To those in Rome it must have seemed absurd that they should take their leadership, guidance and strategy from a poor poet, a bad priest, a skillful Forum politician, a man whose victories—they were sure—had come by luck and chance. Gaul was now the richest of all conquered lands and, by tradition, it was the Senate's right to share the spoils among the nobles. Should the white cock-pigeon alone make this decision? For he had announced that he would be consul again—and if they let him run, they knew, from his first term in office, that he would make his decisions alone.

To Caesar it was even more absurd. He had brought back peace and victory. To make this peace secure, he now required that the Roman state show mercy: to conquered Gauls, to new citizens, to those who had suffered. He required that Rome show gratitude: to his veterans, to his allies. He required, above all, that Rome change; thus, he proposed to run again for the consulship. It could not be, he felt, that these aging, rotted senators, dominated by a faction of a few ancient families, should dispose of a world, for loot and greed, that he had won by risk of life and troops—and which he *knew* he understood better than they. Nor could he accept that the mobs in the Forum, those present in Assembly under the Capitoline Hill, should be the only ones allowed to vote the laws while his soldiers and the farmer families who bred them, equally Roman citizens, who could not afford the trip to Rome, were deprived of the right to vote.

He held at his command the greatest army in the world; no force ever known to war except, perhaps, that of Alexander the Great could until his time equal it; none could match its victories. And yet in Rome, where gratitude should be, was envy. In Rome, where the law bobbed and danced between the roaring of the crowd and the intrigues of the Senate, there was no order except what blade and muscle imposed. In Rome his enemies cited laws by which they might summon him to lay down command and return to face trial before packed juries for indictments yet unframed. And where old laws left loopholes, they now passed laws that reached back years in time to snare him.

There is a magic to the law. One reads Caesar and there is instinct reverence for the law in every line that he writes. But which laws should he accept, and which repudiate? One set of laws gave him every right to run for consul, present or absent; another denied that right.

And what if the old laws were wrong? What then?

What if laws require one to face trial, then, perhaps, die, and one knows the law is being used not as law but as voodoo—and that if one snaps one's finger to set the troops on march, the law is done with?

That was Caesar's problem at the Rubicon.

Insanity, I think, is best defined as a situation where an individual loses contact with reality. It makes no difference what the reality is. If the reality is in itself absurd, if reality is mad, and the individual, judged by normal standards, is sane, then, nonetheless, the individual must be judged mad for rejecting absurd reality.

The political transformation of Caesar *popularis* to Caesar *dictator* happened, I think, at the Rubicon. But to the man personally, more than that probably happened. We have lived and still live in an age when dictators, risen through the people, are carried away to think of themselves as divine, the expression of God's will, or Gods themselves.

Some such transformation of personality under pressure must have happened to Caesar in the few weeks he paused at Ravenna, by the Rubicon, en route home from victory to the expected ceremony of triumph. He returned to his base camp in northern Italy late in 50 B.C. —expecting honor. He found the law prepared against him, and trial impending which might, if he obeyed the summons, bring him shameful exile at the best, death at the worst. He pleaded. He negotiated with those who held the power back in Rome. The last line in his history of the Gallic wars (written by his companion Hirtius) tells of his effort to reach some sort of settlement with the Senate of Rome within the law. The book ends:

". . . *tamen Caesar omnia patienda esse statuit, quoad sibi spes aliqua relinqueretur iure potius disceptandi quam belli gerendi*" ("Nonetheless, Caesar decided to endure all in patience so long as any hope was left to him of settling matters by law, rather than by making war").

But it was not to be. They forced the issue to arms— or perhaps it was he who did so. Students of ancient jurisprudence argue whose guilt it was with as much emotion, today, as men did in 50 B.C.

Whichever way it was, I have done my best to imagine how it may have been in Caesar's mind as he, finally,

came to reject both reality and law. The datings, episodes, programs, negotiations embedded in the essay-
melodrama that follows are as close to accurate as modern scholarship will allow me to be. Yet it must be noted
that though classical scholars have worked on this turbu-
lent six-week period of decision with enormous insight
and diligence, they have never come to any unanimity
on fact, or motivations, or law, or justice.

The words, talk and action of the episode that follows
I have drawn from imagination, skipping as best I could
between the facts on which scholars are agreed.

Villa Serbelloni
Como, Italy
June, 1966

Fair Harbor
Fire Island, New York
October, 1967

CAST OF CHARACTERS

G. JULIUS CAESAR: Imperator. We see him at age 52, en route home from his Gallic triumph, to Rome.

G. ASINIUS POLLIO: Narrator. Later to become a famous general and man of letters. We see him at age 25, a young man of Rome's fashionable literary set, fled to Caesar's camp from scandal in Rome. At Caesar's camp he was headquarters historian and later wrote the famous *Civil Wars*, based on his experiences. Although lost, Pollio's history is considered the chief source for all other ancient accounts of Caesar's triumphs and tragedy.

AULUS HIRTIUS: Caesar's chief of secretariat.

TITUS LABIENUS: Caesar's deputy commander and chief-of-staff in the Gallic campaign. One of Rome's greater military figures, overshadowed in his own time only by Caesar and Pompey.

MARK ANTONY: A youthful Roman soldier and politician. A major figure in the later Civil Wars, future consort of Cleopatra, but at this point achieving his first fame as one of Caesar's lieutenants.

CORNELIUS BALBUS: Spaniard, originally an alien, now a naturalized Roman citizen. He is Caesar's chief agent in the corruption of Roman politics, contact with senatorial intrigue; bagman and briber.

SCRIBONIUS CURIO: Tribune. A key operator in Roman politics. Reportedly bought over to support Caesar's politics some years before the action at the Rubicon, and now Caesar's chief spokesman on the Senate floor.

VERCINGETORIX: Gallic chieftain. Vercingetorix had organized the last great revolt of the Gallic tribes two years before the episode at the Rubicon; was conquered; then surrendered at the siege of Alesia in 52 B.C.; and is now being held for the anticipated triumphal celebration at which he is to be executed.

TAILOR

COMMANDER OF THE GUARD

SOLDIERS

SLAVES

ACT ONE

Narrator begins on forestage in front of curtain, which will slowly open as he talks. Stage will be dim-lit as curtain begins to open, then, when fully open, stage full-lit. Enter narrator—Gaius Asinius Pollio, later to be known as the great historian of the Roman civil wars. We see him, just appointed as scribe in Caesar's Gallic Headquarters, a youth fresh from Rome.

POLLIO: (*As narrator*) Gaius Julius Caesar. (*Fondling each word of the name*) A man to make you wonder. And who's to say the right and wrong of what he did? Or what it cost him? I was twenty-five when he took me on, and he past fifty—and what's twenty-five to know how it aches when you've passed fifty? Whether the Republic had to die? Or whether he really had to break the law? I came to write the true history of the Conquest of the North; Ocean to Sea, Alps to Bay—ruins, smoke, burnt cities, tumbled walls. Nine years of war, but done finally. Fifteen million Gauls, broken by fifty thousand legionaries— and Caesar's will. Never to threaten us again. The fields silent, not a whimper left.

(*Curtain begins to open, stage dark.*)

I met him that autumn in Gaul-Beyond-the-Alps, his victory already sealed by peace. In December—he set out for Gaul-Within-the-Alps. And Italy. And home. Expecting welcome, honor, his parade of triumph.

They waiting for him too—some in joy, some in fear. But most just waiting. The Republic, waiting to know its fate. With all its laws to honor him or break him. For victory had made him big; and time had made him strange—nine long years away. He was still wearing the scarlet cape in the field when I first met him. Only an imperator can wear the scarlet cape, you know. It's the symbol of *imperium*, the power. It gives immunity. No one can bring a man in scarlet cape to trial—he's above the law as long as he holds a fighting command for Rome beyond the pass. He *is* Rome's law. That's clear?

But command was going to expire March first.

(*Stage now lit, curtain open, Pollio steps up to main stage.*)

We'd ridden hard from Gaul to reach rear headquarters, Ravenna. Twenty miles beyond is the pass that separates the province from the Republic. One law there beyond the pass—the law the Senate and Assembly make. Another law here—imperator's law so long as he speaks for the state.

A line between.

And no commander can cross that line with troops except by permission of Senate or Assembly—when triumph brings him home for honor, or crisis brings him back to do the Senate's will. It's tricky. Not clear at all.

(*Pollio mounts the balcony.*)

A little river there marks the boundary line—the Rubicon.

(*Pollio points vaguely south from balcony.*)

You can't see it from here, but it's there. He sent me on ahead this afternoon with Hirtius, his secretary-general, to greet the others. Damned important meeting.

SCENE ONE

T I M E : Late afternoon, December 3, 705 A.U.C. (Ab Urbe Condita—From the Founding of the City), later to be reckoned as the year 50 B.C.

P L A C E : The Praetorium, Caesar's pro-consular winter headquarters at Ravenna, in northern Italy beyond the Rubicon.

As curtain opens, we see an austere timbered background. This is a military headquarters, built of huge timbers. We are in a huge tower-chamber, for Ravenna lies on marshland, and height is necessary for surveillance and sighting of distant hills. Backstage and left, the scene is closed by a semicircle of huge timber pillars that give the effect of opening on a balcony. A low rim, or parapet, on this balcony beyond the timber adds the sense of height. Sentries and lookouts pace it. One can look over the parapet (as several of our characters will do) to see who is approaching from the town or plain below.

Forestage is in sharp contrast with this austere background. The one wall to the set curves from parapet, deep right, to forestage right. It is a glistening white, and dazzling with its display of battle trophies— swords of various curves and lengths; helmets of vari-

ous bulbous shapes; battle-axes; javelins. Roman lamps
on silver standards are lit.

To modern eyes, all Roman interiors appear unfurnished.
A javelin stand is forestage left. But the only piece
of furniture as curtain opens is the "mensa," the
classical low, long, flat Roman table. Caesar's mensa
is covered with snow-white linen, and on it an im-
mense gleaming silver bowl of grapes—white, red,
blue.

Stage has three levels: Low forelevel in front of curtain for narrator. Main level for most of the action.
Slightly higher level for the balcony.

(*Enter two soldiers carrying a magnificent gold stool.
Followed by Commander of the Guard. Followed by
Aulus Hirtius, Caesar's chief secretary. Hirtius is tall,
stooped, irritable. A man of about fifty. He has no
other life but Caesar's wish.*)

HIRTIUS: (*As soldiers set stool down beside the
mensa*) No! Not there! *Behind* the table! It's a rule!
(*As they move it to the side*) No! Blockheads, no!
(*To the Commander*) Where do you get such troops?

COMMANDER: (*Man of about thirty, rough-tongued
field officer*) Field soldiers, sir, not used to headquarters duty.

HIRTIUS: (*Tugging stool into place*) There. Nobody is allowed to sit *behind* Caesar. It's a rule! (*He
fusses over the stool, replacing it.*)

(*Pollio, who has just stepped down from balcony level,
notes this in his tablet. He carries a stylus and a two-
paneled waxed diptych. This is his notetaking pad.
He is constantly jotting notes for his history through-*

out the play.)

POLLIO: Why that rule?

HIRTIUS: (*Ignoring Pollio*) Now the other stools. He'll be here any minute. They'll all be here.

COMMANDER: (*To soldiers*) Jump! Jump to it, lead-butts. He's coming. (*As they leave, he speaks to Hirtius.*) Sir? That crowd downstairs. They've been waiting since morning. They want to know how long they have to wait.

(*Soldiers leave intermittently, return, bearing stools, arranging furniture.*)

HIRTIUS: (*Ignoring the Commander's question*) Is the guard posted?

COMMANDER: Posted.

HIRTIUS: Messenger group ready?

COMMANDER: Ready.

HIRTIUS: Engineers and contractors?

COMMANDER: Sir—*everybody's* here. Petitioners. Claimers. Messengers. Troops. Boiling around downstairs like chickens waiting for a rooster. Lawsuits, dancers, poets, tailors. The poets are the worst; they keep itching at me; they don't like the way it smells downstairs; they say they aren't used to this kind of waiting.

HIRTIUS: (*Snapping*) They'll wait. When Caesar arrives at winter headquarters, he expects everyone to be waiting: bankers, scribes, messengers, tailors, doctors—all waiting. It's a rule. When he knows his mood, he tells me, I tell you, you tell them. Now, these other stools . . .

(*Hirtius busies himself arranging other stools for conference. Commander shrugs and turns confidentially to young Pollio.*)

COMMANDER: Hey—you with the staff?

POLLIO: (*Bowing, dapper, sophisticated. Amused at the manners of the Commander*) G. Asinius Pollio. Headquarters historian. At your service.

COMMANDER: (*Gruffly, acknowledging, it means nothing to him*) Yeah. (*Then, confidentially*) Hey, what the Hell's going on? There's trouble, isn't there?

POLLIO: What trouble?

COMMANDER: (*Irritated*) Everybody's talking. The troops are itching. (*Impatiently*) They've got to get this settled: Do we march to Rome?

POLLIO: Of course. We're here to parade the triumph.

COMMANDER: (*Impatiently*) That's not the way we hear it. Do we get our land?

POLLIO: And how do you hear it?

COMMANDER: That the Senate's relieving Caesar of command. They relieve Caesar—then we don't get our land. Marius' men got land. Sulla's men got land. Pompey's men got land—

POLLIO: (*Flatly*) Caesar's men will get land. He promised. Caesar's running for consul next year. The Senate or Assembly has to pass the law—it's simply a matter of politics.

COMMANDER: (*Interrupting*) Oh, that law stuff again! If we get to march to Rome, we can *vote* ourselves the land. We conquered Gaul. We got the right to march in triumph. They can't stop us.

(*Commander is interrupted by thump of spear as, preceded by a single soldier, Labienus enters in his legate's coat. Labienus is a husky, no-nonsense type. A rigid man with no nicety of expression, no small talk. Commander of the Guard freezes to attention.*)

Pollio takes out his tablet, begins to make notes. Hirtius stops his fussing with table, greets Labienus.)

HIRTIUS: *(Advancing to give dextrum-ad-dextra greeting)* Titus Labienus! Titus Labienus—six months since last we saw each other—

LABIENUS: Eight months—April when I left Gaul to come here. Where is he?

HIRTIUS: He'll be here in minutes now. We rode ahead with the gear.

LABIENUS: *(Snarling)* Then where's Antony? And Balbus? He'll want the news from Rome the minute he gets out of saddle. Jupiter! *I* want the news from Rome. Where *are* they?

HIRTIUS: They came two hours ago. *(To Commander)* Tell Antony and Balbus that the legate has arrived. To come at once.

(Commander leaves, beckons soldiers to come with him, leaving Labienus, Hirtius and Pollio alone.)

HIRTIUS: *(Looking Labienus over)* You look well, Titus Labienus. Seven months of rear duty have fattened you.

LABIENUS: I eat too much. And march too little. I'm not a man for garrison duty—or for judging in provincial courts: land claims, sheep stealing, contractors. *(Shakes his head, makes a grimace.)* Either at the front, or back in Rome—*that's* where a man should be.

HIRTIUS: Well, someone's got to command at the line. Someone Caesar trusts. It's a rule—

LABIENUS: *(Breaking in)* How is he? What's the news in Gaul?

HIRTIUS: Quiet.

LABIENUS: Must be. This time of year he should

be sending captives home for sale. After we took Alesia, two years ago, we got ten slave-trains a day down from Gaul to auction. This year—not one.

HIRTIUS: New rules. He says the Gauls are broken. He calls this the year of clemency. No fighting—so no slaves.

LABIENUS: (*As if uttering a dirty word*) "Clemency." The Senate doesn't like this clemency business. They send their agents here to see me. Fingering at me; trying to finger out his thoughts. Feeling around. We caught one of Cato's spies last week; a slave—we killed him. I know they don't like this clemency talk. They say Caesar got his loot—now no more loot? They want their turn.

HIRTIUS: There's no loot when there's no fighting. It's over—don't they know?

LABIENUS: (*Grumpily*) They're spoiled. They want their share. Everybody wants their share—and they're still mad because of Uxellodunum.

HIRTIUS: That was *last* year, I thought they'd forgotten that.

LABIENUS: They never forget. Five thousand prisoners, healthy Gauls—and he chopped the left hand off every one. Then set them free. Ruined them! Worth a million denarii as slaves—state property, too. The Senate has a case there. Where he gets these new ideas—

HIRTIUS: (*Interrupting*) He's full of new ideas. That's the clemency policy. Surprising how grateful captives are if you set them free. Only you mustn't overdo it—that's why he cut their hands off, a precaution so they couldn't fight again. Going to make citizens of the Gauls, he says; votes for everyone.

Going to change everything once he gets re-elected: new roads, bridges, arenas, courts, marble instead of brick.

LABIENUS: I tell you he goes too fast. Gaul is Gaul, that's conquest. But Rome is Rome. They don't want new ideas in Rome— (*Thump of staff announcing Balbus and Mark Antony.*) That's Antony and Balbus. They're fresh up from Rome. They'll tell you.

(*Enter Mark Antony and Balbus. Antony is a husky, muscular thirty-two, dressed in senatorial toga with thin stripes of purple. Balbus is robed in citizen white. Balbus and Antony talking as they enter—Balbus, swarthy, fat and small, un-Roman, holding the taller by the elbow in conspiratorial gesture of comradeship. There is little warmth in their greetings to Labienus, or his to them, as they give the ceremonial greetings and dextrum-ad-dextra.*)

BALBUS: (*Mincingly*) Greetings, Legate.

ANTONY: (*Booming voice, expansively*) Greetings, Titus Labienus. Greetings, Aulus Hirtius. (*Looks around stage.*) His gear is here, I see. Where's he?

LABIENUS: (*Snapping*) Coming in a minute. You're late. What's news from Rome?

BALBUS: Talk, riot, confusion, debate—the same.

LABIENUS: No. Not the same. Jupiter! This new Senate vote! What's it mean?

BALBUS: (*Soothingly*) It means the Senate's frightened, that's all. They don't know Castor from Pollux, left from right, north from south. It's not a vote—it's a prayer that everyone sit still.

LABIENUS: We *can't* sit still. Time's running against us. The new consuls take office first of January. Our command runs out the first of March. Caesar and I go up as candidates for election in Fifth Month from March. We need a plan—

A N T O N Y : That's why we're here—

L A B I E N U S : (*Wheeling on him*) *You* explain this vote. You and Curio were supposed to work things out in Rome—and then this vote! I thought you had it stopped.

B A L B U S : *We* thought we had it stopped. That was last week. Then the Senate broke and changed its mind—

L A B I E N U S : (*Roaring*) You said you had them bought, *you* did!

B A L B U S : (*Shrugging*) The Senate won't stay bought any more, that's the trouble. They take our money, take Pompey's money, and then—

A N T O N Y : (*Pacing angrily, picking up narrative*)— then they roll in drunk for sessions. And listen to Cato's voice, the voice of virtue, the voice of the fathers, and they cheer him, and—

B A L B U S : —they vote one day this way, the next day the other way. The faction threatens them, Cato yells at them, we pay them, Pompey pays them. This vote came up overnight, like that, the best we could settle for—and swept the floor—

A N T O N Y : —biggest vote in five years, to strip both Pompey and Caesar of their commands. That Senate—wants to crawl back into yesterday, with Pompey and Caesar both forgotten.

L A B I E N U S : (*Storming*) But Curio is tribune. And you take over as tribune next week. Appeal! Take it to the people in Assembly. The Forum's where our vote is—not the Senate.

A N T O N Y : Where our vote used to be, you mean.

LABIENUS: When Caesar and I ran elections, that's where our vote always was.

ANTONY: (*Growing angry himself*) But that was nine years ago, I tell you. (*Pauses at far end of stage, clears his throat, then spits a gobbet of spit in an enormous arc.*) They spit! If they don't like the speakers, they spit. They have squads of spitters now. With a good back-wind, they can spray you at fifty feet. (*Wipes an imaginary spray of spit off his face.*)

BALBUS: Spit—and rocks, and knives, and gangs.

LABIENUS: Don't tell me about voters. Caesar and I *organized* them. The workingmen in *collegia*. The tribes through the bosses. Tickets for the games. Plenty of entertainment—

BALBUS: Plenty of entertainment—but the others have learned the tricks, too—

LABIENUS: (*Ignoring Balbus, for whom he has contempt*) I'm talking. And, on top of that, a few friendly troops in the Forum on election day, to quiet them, a nice orderly vote. (*Emphasizes*) *With troops.*

ANTONY: But the only troops in Rome are Pompey's troops, not ours.

LABIENUS: You say this vote stripped Pompey, too, don't you? Then team with Pompey. It's a simple matter of tactics. Antony, by all the Gods, you have to see it. We make a pact with Pompey, the whole affair is done. Appeal to the people in Assembly. We reverse this vote. Then we get elected. Orderly. By law. Neatly.

ANTONY: That's Caesar's decision—not yours.

BALBUS: (*Soothingly*) That's why we're here, isn't it? To make a plan. When Caesar comes, he'll have a plan. He always has a plan.

LABIENUS: No. He won't. He'll wait to see what happens. He waits, and plays, and jokes. Then, when he strikes—it happens instantly. Thirteen years ago, I remember, we were young then. We got the Assembly to change the law of priests and throw the High Priest's office open to public vote—you remember?

HIRTIUS: I remember. Cicero was consul then.

ANTONY: Cicero—the Gods should strike him dead.

LABIENUS: (*During this speech, he grows moody and, slowly, as he paces, retires to the third tier of the stage, along the parapet, so that the speech closes as if he were far away in place and time.*) Cicero pleaded with Caesar not to mock the holy office— and I thinking Caesar wasn't serious. When Cicero leaves, Caesar tells me he's running himself to be High Priest, Pontifex Maximus. "Caesar," says I, "you can't. High Priest presides over divorces, you've been in every bed in Rome." "Qualifies me, then," says he; "besides, I like the color of the High Priest's robes—saffron. I want to see how I look in saffron." "Be serious," says I. And then he says, "I want to see what happens when I stand alone in Jupiter's Temple at midnight, on the New Year, when Jupiter speaks to the Pontifex Maximus. What does he say? How does God speak?" Our Caesar, I tell you, has no plans. He explores. Never knows what he wants to do until he gets there. Then—strike! War and politics—I've served the man for fifteen years—

(*Sound of cornet directly beneath the parapet. An answering blast of the ram's horn comes from the parapet. All freeze, as Labienus concludes.*)

LABIENUS: —it's all there in his mind, and no one

knows until he peels it out.

(*Hirtius is frantically rearranging the mensa, the stool, the grapes, as the others pleat their togas and pull themselves together.*)

HIRTIUS: (*To Pollio*) Go. Greet him. Tell him all wait.

(*Pollio trips out, gracefully but hastily.*)

LABIENUS: (*Watching Pollio go. Labienus is the only man not rigidly nervous.*) Now, who the Hell is that? He was scribbling down our words all the while we talked. I saw.

HIRTIUS: Name is Pollio. Came on as headquarters reporter two months ago. Harmless.

LABIENUS: No writer's harmless. I don't like them around. People suck up to them just to get their names in books—

BALBUS: That helps sometimes. Helps you with the voters.

LABIENUS: Voters don't read. Games are what they want. Entertainment. And some troops to keep them in order. Not books.

(*Direct blast of trumpet, off-stage, as Caesar enters.*)

(*Caesar is dressed in the scarlet cloak of the proconsular Commander. A gaunt man, sunken cheeks, stern; yet lithe. His stride across the stage is an unbroken flowing motion. As he enters, he is unbuckling his scarlet cape, twirling it so that it flashes brilliantly across the stage. His motion and color are the center of attention and, as if compelled by it, Balbus and Antony dart to catch the cape before it touches the floor.*)

(*Caesar stands for a moment before his stool as they ceremoniously come to attention. Then, since they expect*

it of him, he ceremoniously does the dextrum-ad-dextra grip and returns to the stool. He sags for a moment of weariness, lifts his dirty boots to have them removed, later strapping on the gold-and-crimson thongs of patrician sandals. The soldiers will be helping him and rubbing his legs all through the following sequence until they affix the silver buckles which only patricians wear and then they disappear.)
(Caesar samples a grape—holds the seed delicately in his finger. Balbus rushes over with a tray to catch it. Caesar deposits it neatly, then looks up and smiles for the first time. He gazes at them, who fear him, then shakes his head.)

CAESAR: *(Sardonically)* Caesar's men—the terror of the West. *(Shakes his head again.)* Hirtius!

HIRTIUS: Caesar!

CAESAR: Who waits for attention?

HIRTIUS: Labienus, legate commanding. Antony and Balbus fresh from Rome. Petitioners. Lawsuits on appeal from the whole Po valley. Staff of the Thirteenth Legion. Commander of the Guard. Tailors, poets, engineers, contractors, others.

CAESAR: *(Munching another grape, very slowly, as they all watch him. Delicately and slowly rearranges the grapes over the bowl himself, as if running the names through his mind. Then, crisply commanding)* Lawsuits, petitioners, claimants—dismiss until next week. Staff of the Thirteenth, engineers and Commander of the Guard—all to report to Labienus. But later. The tailors and poets to stay for now. Keep them. Now—*(His eye, scanning them, settles on Mark Antony.)* Mark Antony, tribune-elect! You left Rome when?

ANTONY: Three days ago—as soon as we had your call.

CAESAR: And matters there?

(*Antony, Balbus, Labienus answer almost simultaneously.*)

ANTONY: They want to fight, that's the long and short of it—

BALBUS: They're frightened, every man of them is scared—

LABIENUS: Pompey has the key, I tell you—

CAESAR: Very clear. Let's start again. Antony—you say they want to fight. With whom?

ANTONY: With us.

LABIENUS: No—that's not the way I read it.

CAESAR: (*Cutting in*) I speak to Antony—*who* wants to fight?

ANTONY: The Senate.

BALBUS: No, the Senate is afraid. The families that own the Senate, the *nobiles, they* want to fight. The Senate simply wants its share—without the fighting.

ANTONY: *Cato* wants to fight! He holds the Senate in his hand.

CAESAR: Every band of scoundrels must front itself with at least one honest man—preferably a stupid one. So—Marcus Porcius Cato, guardian of the law, voice of virtue. Wrong at every turn for fifteen years. Yet even he must have a legal reason. What's his reason?

ANTONY: Says Caesar plans to march on Rome with all his legions. Says Caesar's grown too great, must learn obedience to the Senate and Republic like every other citizen—

LABIENUS: Now how, by Jupiter, can Cato say that? Everyone knows our dispositions—four legions with Trebonius, two months' march away, watching Germans. Four legions with Fabius, a month's march away, at Lyons, watching Gauls. This one single legion stretched all across the Po valley. The Senate *knows* it.

CAESAR: So. But supposing Cato was right. With what would he fight my march?

ANTONY: With Pompey's troops—

CAESAR: Pompey. Old Pompey. Balbus—are you in touch with Pompey?

BALBUS: In touch, yes. In contact, no. Who can talk to Pompey? One needs a ladder to reach his ear. And I am Spanish-born, still alien, he thinks. When we meet—he sends you greetings, then . . . talks of his diet.

CAESAR: (*Slowly coming alert at the touch of gossip*) His diet? He has another new cure?

BALBUS: He's dieting again. This new marriage is too much for him—she thirty-eight and ripe for passion, he fifty-six. He'll never make a baby on her. He sleeps with actresses again—it's the talk of town—to keep his courage up.

CAESAR: (*Stretching out, relaxed at last*) Poor Pompey—still with actresses? A young man's sport. I never did enjoy actresses. No talk, just exercise.

ANTONY: (*Falling into the mood*) But actresses are so uncomplicated, Caesar—and what's to talk about in bed?

CAESAR: Ah, Rome, Rome—a glorious city wasted on men like you. Why, Antony—to sleep with slaves or actresses in Rome is wasting its best talent. Actually, a fine, well-bred Roman matron, weary of her husband, trying to find somewhere else the ecstasy he promised, chasing a fading dream—Antony—out there when a woman is reaching through you for what does not exist, more naked in spirit than in body, as she strives and hunts . . . you learn so much about a man by sleeping with his wife. Actually, I first got to understand old Pompey by sleeping with his Mucia; then it pricked his dignity, and he divorced her. I've missed Rome . . . and the stage; and the games; and the banquets; and the ladies . . . how's Servilia?

LABIENUS: (*Breaking in, barely controlling his exasperation*) Caesar!

CAESAR: (*Suddenly grave, turns, voice droops*) Titus Labienus! Titus Labienus, my chief-of-staff! (*Softly, with foreboding, he repeats*) Speak, Titus Labienus!

LABIENUS: Are we gathered to gossip of women? When we have not seen Caesar for months? When matters boil and the afternoon courier, this *very* afternoon, tells us that the Senate—

CAESAR: (*Picking up the phrase*) —that the Senate by a vote of three hundred seventy to twenty-two has resolved that Gaius Julius Caesar and Gnaeus Pompeius Magnus should each give up their armies and commands.

BALBUS: (*Startled*) You know already?

CAESAR: I heard. As I came through the gate, minutes ago. But that is all I heard—what more is there?

BALBUS: We have the vote-count, no more.

CAESAR: News then only of a vote-count. Fact without its echo. When does the next rider come?

BALBUS: Tomorrow. Curio from Rome sends two

couriers a day, at dawn and dusk, to reach here two
days later, at dawn and dusk.

CAESAR: (*Musing*)   A tally. Three hundred seventy
to twenty-two. Numbers can be so treacherous without their meaning.

BALBUS: The meaning is what we make of it, Caesar. Now we have a little time for maneuver. (*He
makes a rubbing motion with his hand, bargaining—
then wriggles.*) It was the best bargain we could get.

CAESAR: With all that you and Curio spent?

BALBUS: With all we spent. There's no honor left,
Caesar. I don't mind bribing a senator who honestly
disagrees with us. You have to pay high when you
buy a man's conscience. But when someone holds
you up for money to vote the way he wants to vote
anyway—it's unethical.

CAESAR: But it lasts longer that way.

BALBUS: Lasts longer that way. That's what I mean.
We bought an honest vote.

LABIENUS: I still don't know what you and Curio
bought.

BALBUS: Confusion. It means the Senate is afraid—
and says so honestly. Wants both Pompey *and* Caesar
to lay down command. Now we have an opening
to reach a bargain with Pompey. He has to listen.
(*Proudly*)

LABIENUS: Then right away, I say. If we have
Pompey with us, let Cato and the noble families blow
which way they will. With Pompey on our side, we'll
get an open vote this summer. What's clearer?

ANTONY: What's clearer? I'll tell you: Rome is
naked. Garrison troops. Old veterans. Pompey's new
recruits. Give me this one legion—give me just one

cohort of this legion marching in triumph, chanting Caesar's name through the streets of Rome— (*Snaps his fingers.*) —we could change it all.

CAESAR: (*Languidly reaches to the table, as he talks, and pulls to him his silver dicing cup.*) But there's no sport in that, Antony. To do it with the legionary's sword. It's so easy that way. Like loaded dice. (*Rolls the dice, gathers them in.*) The trick is harder, but more gay when you *persuade* the voters. And these are Roman voters. Sheeplike, simple, stupid men. But once they vote, the law's a law, the candidate becomes a consul and speaks for Rome. A mob's a mob until it votes; and then a magic rises from their vote. But one must gamble on the vote. (*Rolls again.*)

ANTONY: Gambling's for games. Election's eight months off. And the Senate doesn't want to gamble. If they control the mobs, or Pompey's troops control—how does Caesar get elected? Caesar without his legions is like a crab in molting season, defenseless. We go with troops. Then vote our troops—and *that's* the way.

LABIENUS: You mean cross the Rubicon without permission? One step over and we're outlaws. Then Cato really has us on the law—

ANTONY: Caesar's Gallic legions outlaws? By Hercules, they'd cheer us town by town as we marched on—

LABIENUS: Or fight us step by step. It's the law, by Jupiter, Antony, you know it as well as I. They'd call on Pompey to stop us. Then he'd *have* to fight us. We fight Pompey?! *I* fight Pompey?! And even if we won—we'd have to rewrite every law in Rome.

ANTONY: Why not? The law is cut to fit their will,

the thirty families who think they own the Senate. They loan the law out like a killer's blade. The Senate urged the law on Cicero to kill my stepfather. Legal as could be. But he's dead. (*Antony pulls sword out of scabbard and gently swings it back and forth.*) This makes laws, *this*. (*Softly*) If we moved now, while they were talking.

(*Caesar walks quietly over to Antony, lifts Antony's sword hand, examines the sword, pulls out his own, then, as all watch, gravely measures his own blade against Antony's.*)

CAESAR: Same length. Your sword and mine. Same length. But this . . . (*Crossing stage to take trophy sword from wall*) . . . is Spanish. Longer. Sharper. Better steel. And this . . . (*Taking another sword from wall, thrusting it at Antony's middle, who backs away*) . . . is German. Heavier. You can hack with it. And there . . . (*Taking a pike from the wall, hurling it into wall so that it quivers*) . . . is the Gallic lance. Better than ours. Soft iron—the shaft bends when it hits a shield. You can't pull it out, or hurl it back. . . . And the Balearici are better slingers. The Cretans better archers. The Gauls better horsemen. In Britain, they even fight from carts. And what have we? (*Caesar whirls on Antony, pulling his sword as he whirls.*) What have we except a short sword, a long javelin, a heavy shield, a trenching shovel—and a dagger for the officers? What else, Antony? What conquered Hannibal, Macedon, Spain, Syria, Gaul, the Germans? (*The sword in Caesar's hand lowers with a slow menacing fall, pointing to Antony's belly. Antony backs away.*) What, Antony?

ANTONY: The legions and the Gods.

CAESAR: But what *made* the legions? The Germans
and Gauls are bigger and stronger than we are. The
Greeks and Jews have cleverer Gods. What gave
Rome victory? (*All are silent.*) The law! Four hundred and fifty years of law! The law makes the legions. The law binds Roman to Roman—that each
man stand in battle line, facing forward, knowing he
must die for his fellow on right or left because his
fellow will die for him. Four hundred and fifty years
of law—legionary standing in obedience to centurion,
because he knows his centurion obeys the legate, the
legate the commander, the commander the laws of
Rome. The law mounting to the Temple of Jupiter,
where it binds man in the order of the immortal
Gods. And you say we should break the law? Four
hundred and fifty years of the Republic, all its conquests—rest on law. Break it?

LABIENUS: How's that, O Tribune? Answer that
one.

ANTONY: (*Scowling, unhappy, but stubborn*)   Well,
but what if the law wants you dead?

CAESAR: Then we must change it—or find a way
around it. Break it openly? What then? If *we* break
it, others can break the laws *we* plan to pass. Teach
people they need obey no laws except what pleases
them and nothing's left but rabble. There's the problem—how to *act*, yet appear to act by law as well.

LABIENUS: That's the way it has to be. Eight months
to elections. Pompey joins us. We get elected and pass
the laws the way we want.

CAESAR: (*Turning full on Labienus*)   So simple?

We hold command by law until the first of March—
but between the first of March and Fifth Month
later, it's they who hold the courts—

ANTONY: And Cato swears as soon as Caesar drops
the scarlet cloak, he'll stand him up for trial.

LABIENUS: Try Caesar? For what?

CAESAR: (*Sitting. Voice changing. Talks as if impersonally talking of a third person, pointing an
accusatory finger at an imaginary Caesar.*) Indict
Caesar for needless war in Gaul—then the Senate
soothes its conscience by convicting Caesar and keeping Gaul as spoils to boot. Or—the gifts Caesar won
in Gaul; call it extortion. Or: rejection of Senate advice—call it treason. Or, simple adultery; a dozen
cuckolds in that Senate will sacrifice their wives'
honor to see me guilty.

LABIENUS: But we are victors, Caesar, we are heroes
—we come from Gaul in triumph!

CAESAR: But what if sometime between the first of
March, when command expires, and when we run
for consulate, Senate or court proclaims me outlaw—
where is Labienus?

LABIENUS: Where am I? Caesar?! With you! As
last year in Belgium; the year before at Alesia; five
years ago at the Channel; as next year in Rome, running together as partners for the consulate—

CAESAR: (*Rising, crossing to Labienus, slowly, prose-
cuting, demanding answers*) Where are you, Titus
Labienus, if the law proclaims me outlaw?

LABIENUS: Then we are both outlaws.

CAESAR: Let me make it clearer. If Cato's court
names only Caesar outlaw, leaving Labienus to choose

between Caesar and the law?

ANTONY: How's that, O Chief-of-Staff? You answer that one!

LABIENUS: (*Venting his irritation on Antony because he dare not vent it on Caesar*) Caesar toys with me—and you feed his game! No one, no Roman living or dead, no tribune, senator, general, not even Pompey can match our triumphs. Who dares deny Caesar his honor, forbid his rights to stand for office?

CAESAR: Unless they prove Caesar has broken law—

ANTONY: (*Rubbing it in*) —and this new law says you must give up command.

CAESAR: Not clear at all. *This* week's Senate says I must give up command. Nine years ago the Senate's law gave me Gaul-Beyond-the-Alps. And the Assembly's law gave me Gaul-Within-the-Alps. Laws change fast. Nor do we know when I must give up command. The old law gave us till March the first. So we must wait.

ANTONY: For what, Caesar, for what?

CAESAR: To know the sense of Rome. We have facts that masquerade as news; a single vote ripped out of a dangerous day—two days ago. We need to know the talk— (*Abruptly, turning, cutting off the meeting*) Hirtius!

HIRTIUS: Caesar!

CAESAR: Dismiss for now. I'll bathe. Then have the tailors ready. Then we'll meet again tonight—with song, and poets, and talk—

LABIENUS: Caesar! We've settled nothing. We need a plan. They in Rome—

CAESAR: (*Commanding*) Labienus—meet with the staff of the Thirteenth Legion, have them ready for meeting in the morning at sixth hour. Join me for dinner tonight. And Balbus. And Antony. Join me. After tomorrow's courier we'll know the after-talk in Rome. . . . Dismiss.

(*Exit Labienus, Balbus, Antony.*)

CAESAR: (*Turning to Hirtius*)   And note the interesting cases that wait for settlement; list them all; divorces first, I need amusement; even provincial divorces are amusing; then citizenship cases. Let Labienus handle contracts, land cases. And tailors ready once I've bathed.

(*Exit Hirtius.*)

CAESAR: (*Notices Pollio scribbling notes.*)   You find Caesar interesting, Pollio? It will make a book?

POLLIO: Oh yes, Caesar—oh yes.

CAESAR: (*Lifting Pollio's tablet from his hand*)   You write in Greek? Why not Latin?

POLLIO: But history's always Greek, sir—the best history, that is. The language sings, sir, all elegant histories are Greek.

CAESAR: Too much symmetry in Greek; the words too clear. All black, all white, all heroes, traitors, tyrants. It's not that way at all. (*Caesar clicks and returns the waxed tablet.*)   Write in Latin. A choppy language. But our own.

POLLIO: How's Latin different?

CAESAR: The Greeks believe in fate. But history is chance. Fate is yesterday's chance once you've seen the dice roll. The Greeks have Gods as heroes; we Romans serve our Gods as contract partners. . . .

POLLIO: Yes, sir. . . . (*Waits.*)   Do you need anything, sir, may I bring you anything, sir?

CAESAR: No . . . except your history six months

hence, to say what Caesar's done.

POLLIO: Sir . . . But things seem straight enough. Either Antony's way—by marching; or Labienus' way, by seeking Pompey's help. . . . Sir? Either way we win.

CAESAR: Win what? . . . Nothing's straight, Pollio. (*He makes an elaborate tracing circular motion with his finger.*)

Life winds in spirals.

(*He rises, tracing with his finger.*)

When young, it's straight—people can give you things you want.

(*Spirals again with his finger on a higher level.*)

Then—older? You take the things you want.

(*Traces again.*)

But, always, you know the name of someone who can give, or someone you can raid. Then—finally—when no one's left to give what most you seek, and no one you can raid. Then—what? What can be won by winning, I've already won: consul, money, trophies, victory.

There's Caesar—(*Mimicking*) High Priest.

There's Caesar—praetor, presiding over court.

There's Caesar—politician; orator; poet; gamesman.

There's Caesar—consul, making law.

There's Caesar—conqueror.

And, now, Caesar—tired: of blood, of killing, of victory, of words.

Caesar can have whatever he wants. Except Rome cannot give it, on Rome's terms. Or, perhaps, it can. You see, it's chance, not fate, that governs men. It's not that straight.

(*Circles with his finger.*)

Not straight at all. To yield—is easy. To kill—much easier. To change—change Rome. That's hard. You have to see round corners. For that, one needs the height of Gods.

(*Caesar leaves as Pollio scribbles.*)

CURTAIN

SCENE TWO

(*Enter Pollio, in front of curtain, which will open about
halfway through his narration.*)

POLLIO: (*As narrator*) In school, they taught us
simple answers: *Populus Senatusque Romanus*—Sen-
ate-and-People-of-Rome were one. People in Assembly in the Forum elected the two consuls. The consuls, with advice and consent of the Senate proposed
laws to people in Assembly. Assembly voted the laws,
up or down. When they voted war, they voted themselves to march. All made the laws, so all obeyed. And
the courts protected every citizen by open trial in
the forum.

Neat. So neat in schoolbooks.

Only . . . now . . .

Rome's bursting . . . has been bursting for fifty
years, an age of triumph . . . and disaster. Too
many victories. Too much money. Frontiers too far
away to understand . . . Forum mobs who've never
seen a battle voting armies into being who've never

gazed on Rome . . . Laws proposed direct to Assembly without consent of Senate . . . The Senate,
an old man's club, cowed by the *nobiles,* whose ancient family names—Scipios, Caecili-Metelli, Domitii,
Aemilii, Porci-Catones, Livii, Junii—are carved on
every public building. Every one jealous of *his* rights,
his privileges. The Senate for its honor and its wealth;
the army and their leaders for dignities and loot; the
mob for bread—and citizens' seats at games. All the
ancient rituals preserved—but no logic to it any more.
And Caesar?

Caesar loved the ritual; but had an appetite for logic,
too, a passion almost.

(*Curtain has opened meanwhile on the same scene, only
now a long table has replaced the mensa; and the tailor, with two assistants, is arranging brilliantly colored
cloths on the table. All through the following action,
these brilliant cloths will be flashing in the background as the tailor's assistants display them. Now
Pollio steps into the action, as Commander of the
Guard enters.*)

COMMANDER: Caesar comes!

(*Enter Caesar, in his scarlet cloak at which the tailor and
his two assistants immediately bow their heads. Caesar
is followed by Pollio.*)

TAILOR: (*Bowing low with an Oriental sweep*)   Imperator! Great Caesar! What honor to be called from
Rome to serve you.

CAESAR: Welcome, tailor. (*Then, ignoring him,
turns to Pollio.*) Clothes are so important.

POLLIO: Sir?

CAESAR: In Rome, I mean. Clothes cast the role—
senator, tribune, general, priest, candidate. People

must recognize the role before they know the man—like masks in tragedies. (*Turning to tailor*) Let's see your stuffs. (*Turning back to Pollio*) Rome has not seen me for nine full years. The clothes must match their dreams or fears. (*To tailor*) Well, tailor?

TAILOR: Which colors first, O Caesar?

CAESAR: Commanders' scarlet. (*Examining a bolt on the table*) A little off-color this, isn't it?

TAILOR: (*Unrolling the bolt so that the colors splash on stage*) No. It's the style . . . a bit more vermilion in the scarlet these days. Takes getting used to . . . (*Matches the new scarlet against Caesar's old scarlet.*) . . . and the cloak you have is faded.

CAESAR: Scarlet fades when you wear it in the field . . . rain and sun; mudstains and blood; sweat from the horses. Yes . . . for parades, scarlet should be fresh, the way the people like to see it. Not dirty as in battle.

TAILOR: (*Diffidently*) Also, they pinch the waist a bit these days. Let me drape this on . . . if . . . if Imperator would drop his toga.

(*Caesar drops his cloak, reveals the Roman undershirt. But the Roman undershirt, unlike Roman custom, is stuffed into Gallic woolen trousers. The tailor stares, draws back.*)

CAESAR: What are you gawking at, tailor?

TAILOR: Imperator?! (*Points at the trousers, then pulls at his crotch.*) Those?

CAESAR: Breeches, tailor, Gallic breeches—cut off a bit at the knees. Have you seen none before?

TAILOR: I've heard them talk of Gallic breeches. But I've never seen them. Do they hurt? Don't they grab you here? (*Clutches again at his groin.*)

CAESAR: No.

POLLIO: But, sir? I know that women wear them now in Rome. It's all the fashion. But men are different, you know, sir, don't they pinch?

TAILOR: (*Shaking his head*) For field campaigning, I suppose, they may be useful—but not for use in Rome, I hope.

CAESAR: (*Exasperated*) To wear whenever I want. They keep me warm. It's easier in the saddle. No wind blows to chill me. A Gallic custom and a good one. The Gauls have many customs we can take. Like mattresses to sleep on. Better than boards.

TAILOR: But . . . they spoil the line. (*Appealing to Pollio*) Do they not?

CAESAR: (*Annoyed*) Come, let's get on with it.

TAILOR: (*Placating*) For older men, I mean, it might spoil the line, when they go to fat. But Imperator has the waist and bearing of a man of thirty.

CAESAR: There's time to flatter me when we start to fit. Let's see the stuffs first. I need a new scarlet for the triumph. Two of them. Then some saffrons.

POLLIO: I've never seen a saffron robe.

CAESAR: Quite right. Only the High Priest wears all saffron. (*Tailor is unrolling saffron bolts in another splash of color as Caesar talks.*) And I am High Priest still, though nine long years away. Rome will want to see its High Priest home again, robed all in saffron, a sight for youngsters, a holy man. (*Laughs and makes the upturned-palms gesture of the Roman priest.*) I like to play that role. (*Turns on tailor.*) But that's not saffron. That's yellow. Sickish.

TAILOR: (*Rippling another sheet before him*) This?

CAESAR: Too orange. I want saffron, real saffron,

color of the bride and sacrament. Two of them, lest one stain at sacrifice. (*To Pollio*) People enjoy ceremonies. Old folk explain it to children. They watch. They want the colors precise, exact. In temple, they'll forgive anything but off-color ritual. In politics, too— Tailor! The whites for candidates?

T A I L O R :   The whites, sir. . . . (*Spreading them*)

C A E S A R :   (*Examining, explaining to Pollio*) No choice for fashion here. The candidates wear white . . . for purity. White wool, by custom.

P O L L I O :   Sir—some are wearing white in silk in Rome these days.

C A E S A R :   So? All silk, then, tailor. I am candidate for consul once again come summer. Candid white for candidates . . . and I will have all silk—right, Pollio?

P O L L I O :   Oh, marvelous . . . to shimmer when you walk and speak.

T A I L O R :   But it takes months to gather all that silk, then spin and weave it. . . .

C A E S A R :   You have time. All silk. And then a new consular robe for after election. White wool with purple silk as border!

T A I L O R :   I have the stuffs for consular robes.

(*As his assistants unroll bolts of cloth and flash them through the air, one notices they are white striped with a broad band of purple. At this point, in the distance the sound of a horn announces a new arrival.*)

T A I L O R :   You will notice, Imperator, that the consulars are wearing a broader band of purple on their robes than when last you held the office . . . the styles change in nine years.

C A E S A R :   More than style has changed.

P O L L I O :   (*Examining a bolt*) What a beautiful color

purple is. Do you ever make all purple robes?

TAILOR: Only for foreigners. Eastern kings who bring tribute to the Senate. For these we make purple edged in gold. For all others—it is forbidden. (*Unraveling a bolt of purple*) This is how it looks—

CAESAR: (*Snapping*) Away with that, fool! Fold it! (*To Pollio, angrily*) No Roman has worn purple in four hundred and fifty years. It's the color of kings. All it needs is for one of Cato's spies to whisper in Rome that Caesar's tailor measures him for purple— (*To tailor*) Tailor! How long will it take to spin, weave, dye, cut the robes?

TAILOR: But which first, Caesar? When does Caesar go to Rome? And how? As imperator in combat scarlet? Or as priest in saffron? Or as candidate in white?

CAESAR: Tailor, tailor—if I could answer your question, if any man could answer, Rome and I together would pay you any ransom—

(*Enter Hirtius, agitated.*)

HIRTIUS: Caesar! Another messenger from Curio in Rome. Exhausted. He broke two horses on the way— fresh news. (*Turns to tailor.*) Out! Out! All of you! Caesar must be alone!

(*A frantic bustle and confusion follow as tailor and slaves bundle all their cloths into a tumbled heap, backing away. Caesar gravely observes them. Quite serene, he goes on talking.*)

CAESAR: Do not hurry, tailor. The news is two days old—whatever it is. And thank you, tailor. Until tomorrow. Start the saffron first, but real saffron. That's safe enough—no one but the Gods can relieve their High Priest of command. (*As stage clears, leaving*

Caesar with Pollio and Hirtius, he is still unruffled.)
What kind of message? Code or plain?

HIRTIUS: In code. Balbus is working it out now.
It's short.

CAESAR: In code—bad news. If good—Curio would
have written plain.

HIRTIUS: Should we call the others? Antony? Labienus?

CAESAR: No. I'll take the message first. Where's
Balbus? (*Enter Balbus with pad.*) Let's have it.

BALBUS: (*Beginning to read*) "Curio to Caesar.
Greetings. Si tu vales—"

CAESAR: Skip the greetings.

BALBUS: (*Scanning hastily*) Oh, here . . . it starts.
. . . "Rome. Written at midnight. The vote has
been reversed. . . ."

HIRTIUS: They can't reverse a vote that fast—

POLLIO: But the afternoon courier said it was three
hundred seventy to twenty-two. How—

CAESAR: Quiet. Let Curio speak. Go on, Balbus.

BALBUS: (*Continuing*) "Marcellus, outgoing consul, declares he cannot in his last three weeks of office
ignore his duties. Thus, in duty, he feels he must
ignore the Senate's morning vote. Our spies report:
Marcellus has gathered friends this night and told
them: All nine of Caesar's legions and his Gauls are
now assembling at Ravenna to march on Rome. Curio
has denied this, but asks of Caesar swift reply whether
this be true."

POLLIO: It's a lie!

CAESAR: Quiet! Go on!

BALBUS: (*Continuing to read the message*) "Marcellus insists while he remains consul he must defend

the city. And thus has gone this evening to visit Pompey, asking that he, Pompey, assume defense to protect the law against its enemies. At late hour, after conference, Pompey and Marcellus send messages. Marcellus calls the Senate to meet again tomorrow in Pompey's villa outside the wall. Each senator called for tenth hour to safeguard the state and reconsider votes. If they repeal the vote . . . what then? Curio waits Caesar's instructions. Salutes."

CAESAR: So . . . it clears. I knew they would not stick to it. Marcellus is the tool of the *nobiles*. Cato is their emblem. They bend the laws; and all they need are troops. They wish to contract with Pompey before we can. Use his troops. Strip me of mine. . . .

POLLIO: But they can't make one law this morning, another tomorrow.

CAESAR: Yes, they can. In state emergency, a consul has the right to act alone if need be. I did. Marcellus cries: Invasion. If Italy is invaded by Caesar, he must protect the Republic. So, name by name, he will call the roll, saying: Speak. And each will stand to give assent.

HIRTIUS: But there *is* no emergency.

CAESAR: If the *nobiles* can persuade Pompey to see it as emergency, describe his duty . . . Pompey has troops . . . troops around the Senate could make the Senate reverse itself and see emergency, too.

BALBUS: The Roman Senate. Cattle turning backs to wind. Five hundred frightened men—terrified—

CAESAR: Of what?

BALBUS: Of you and Pompey—both, equally. And must choose one.

CAESAR: But to fear Pompey and Caesar equally—

folly! I have the Gallic legions at my call.

BALBUS: Pardon, Caesar. You have the distant sword,
Pompey the near one.

CAESAR: (*Not listening—cutting in*) Balbus! I hear
them talking now in Rome, I hear their gossip in my
ears. It will take days before they reach arrange-
ments. Caesar's voice must be in Rome at once—

BALBUS: To say?

CAESAR: (*Pacing, intent*) To promise promises, to
make accommodation. To drive a wedge between
settlements. What if I yield them what they want—
Gaul to the great families, dignity to Pompey, asking
only my share in return?

BALBUS: Which is?

CAESAR: (*Very firmly*) What the law promises:
the right to stand again for consul come Fifth Month
from March, the people voting openly, what Pompey
promised me two years ago.

BALBUS: But that is what they fear the most, Caesar
—Caesar consul again.

HIRTIUS: Caesar consul again! Caesar as consul pro-
poses laws—and what laws, changes, novelties Caesar
may cause the Assembly to pass, they, the Senate,
will by oath be bound to accept. Pompey dreams no
longer—the Senate can give him what he wants.
What Caesar dreams—they do not know, they are
afraid.

CAESAR: I've said it clear. They know. I have promises to keep—land for my troops. Citizenship for the
Po valley men. Peace for the Gauls—

HIRTIUS: Then—citizenship for Gauls? For Spaniards? Jews? Egyptians? This is what they fear—you
see them from across the mountains like any other

people, Rome another city in a world that's ruled by
Caesar.

CAESAR: (*Ignoring Hirtius. His mind's made up.
Turns to Balbus.*)   You go to Rome tomorrow!

BALBUS: But I just came— I go to Rome again—to
do what?

CAESAR: To bargain. To the Senate—coo. Suck.
Gentle. Gentle, ever so gentle. Money if necessary.
Gifts for their ladies. Erase their fears. Let them
know: Caesar stands alone, with one legion south of
the Alps, of which one cohort only, six hundred men,
camp at Ravenna. And to Pompey, our old friend—

BALBUS: If he will only talk as man to man—

CAESAR: He *must* talk. To Pompey—sterner. Say:
after he returned from Asia, and *I* was consul nine
years ago—I forced the Senate to meet his promises,
land for *his* troops, ratification of *his* peace in the
East. He owes me that much in return.

BALBUS: (*Puffing out his chest, waddling*)   If I were
Caesar, I could say it that way. But I am Balbus. (*He
puts his hand out to show how small he is.*)   I must
creep around—it's difficult to deliver ultimatums on
your knees.

CAESAR: Say it any way you will—on bended knee,
or horseback. Plead. You are no greater man than
Caesar, and *Caesar* pleads. Flatter Pompey. Say that
I crave advice. That always flatters stupid men—

BALBUS: (*Repeating*)   Oh right, oh right, O Caesar
—to flatter him, flattery for stupid men the only
way—oh right—

CAESAR: Don't flatter me. You have it clear: Divide
them, feel them out, what do they feel they need?
But give me room to act.

BALBUS: Divide: Pompey from Senate, Senate from Pompey, *nobiles* from rank-and-file, Senate from Assembly.

CAESAR: No. Antony will handle the Assembly if we must appeal to the Forum. Antony's tribune-elect. To call the mob to action means we call for blood. We do it only if we must—and that's for Antony. *You* go to talk peace—with Pompey, or the *nobiles,* or both. But one thing must be clear: the pledge of one, or another, or all, that come Fifth Month I run for consul in open election with no law to bar me, no fear of trial. Go, now. (*Caesar rises, puts hand firmly on Balbus' shoulder, and walks him to the exit, as Pollio and Hirtius follow.*) I'm cold. (*Hirtius claps hands. Two soldiers enter. Hirtius gives them curt command as Caesar muses.*) It's colder here in the marshes than up north in Gaul. Winter is dry in the north.

HIRTIUS: They will bring warming pans and lamps; but you should rest.

CAESAR: I want to rest in Rome. I've had enough of army camps. I want to be in Rome. (*Pause.*) I think of Rome as warmth and sun. (*To Pollio*) It's good to be in Rome, isn't it?

POLLIO: But, sir . . . this is exciting.

CAESAR: What Rome could be . . . is more exciting. Spring and summer. Woman singing. Children playing. Children run away from me in Gaul. But Rome—the way Polybius wrote of it. No one afraid of street or law. All battle done. The way it used to be, but different. To be the way it used to be—it must be different. But how to make it so? (*Soldiers enter, bringing a brazier of coals, and place it before Cae-*

sar, who warms his fingers over it and cracks his knuckles.) What should I do?

HIRTIUS: What you will do.

CAESAR: You know?

HIRTIUS: No one *knows* what Caesar will do.

CAESAR: Pollio. He knows. He will write it down.

POLLIO: Sir—I'm headquarters reporter. I'll write it down as soon as you tell me.

CAESAR: Everyone else knows what I should do. Labienus knows. Antony knows. The Senate knows. The ladies of Rome know. But only little schoolboys who read Pollio will know what Caesar really did. That is—if Caesar wins. History belongs to winners. Otherwise, Pollio, your time's been wasted. (*Caesar paces.*) Battle's so easy. There are rules. And every rule calls for attack. But this is politics. No logic to it. Nothing talks to me except to say: absurd.

HIRTIUS: What's absurd?

CAESAR: All of it. Rome. Their grandfathers made Rome great. Too great for them to understand. Cato's great-grandfather, the censor: *Delenda est Carthago* was all he knew. Right. Sounded right. Was right— a time for cruelties and punishment. But old Cato plowed in the field, in the sun, naked to his waist, a village chieftain till the day he died. And now Rome's not a village. And his great-grandson thirsts for my blood not because his name's Cato and mine Caesar. But because I cannot see how his village rules can rule the world that Rome has made. (*Speaks as if standing apart, looking down on the pit in the forum.*) You squeeze the villagers through their files. Old Cato used to count the vote by name, when men pro- claimed their vote aloud. And now they vote on tablets, secret tablets dropping in the baskets. So you must reach the hearts you cannot reach through fear. But why—why only in Rome? Why should all the laws of all the world be made there between two hills, Capitoline and Palatine?

HIRTIUS: But that's the rule. Rome is where Assembly always meets. Only in Rome. That's the rule.

CAESAR: Rule! Rule! Rule! But why? Why? Why? Thirty thousand in Assembly and *they* should pass the laws for Gaul and Greece. And the beggars. Garlic on their breath, a silver penny in their pocket, gold for the tribal leaders. Bought. And on a rainy day, only ten thousand come to vote—if you pay them. I *bought* from the Assembly the laws that gave me command in this Po valley. Ten thousand silver pennies only—because it was a rainy day. I killed ten thousand Gauls in Brittany in one week's fighting. I have five times that number in my legions. Citizens all. Who cannot vote unless they get to Rome—who fight but cannot speak, unless Assembly or the Senate gives me leave to bring them home to vote. Rules!

HIRTIUS: But there have to be rules.

CAESAR: So the rules must change.

HIRTIUS: Sulla tried to change the rules.

POLLIO: My grandfather was Italian. He was killed by Sulla. But my father was a citizen—Roman.

HIRTIUS: Sulla killed Romans, too. Forced Assembly to make him Dictator—and there are old men in the Senate still who remember when Sulla called them into session. Down the hill they could hear the screaming as his soldiers killed and stabbed and speared his prisoners. Romans all. They killed all afternoon. The Senate does not want to see rules changed again. They are afraid.

CAESAR: He did not have to kill so much. So soft a voice he had, that Sulla. He almost understood.

POLLIO: (*Scribbling   furiously*) Sir—understood what?

CAESAR: About killing. I was eighteen—younger than you, Pollio—when he had me there before him. I, married to Cornelia, Cinna's daughter; and Cinna murdered by Sulla's rage. Sulla wanted me to divorce Cornelia to prove my loyalty, and marry—who it was I now forget. But I loved Cornelia. Had I been two years older, wiser—I would have left her. Had I been two years older, he would have killed me for refusal—

POLLIO: But—he let you go?

CAESAR: (*Acting it out impersonally*) Let me go. I can see myself. He, sitting there. Holding me before him. Scratching—he had the itch disease, you know, picked it up in Asia. But holding me. It's like the feel of a bird, beating its wings for life in the cup of your hand, when you hold a man like that. When you let the bird go—you score. So Sulla let me go. To please himself. Only to please himself. A man of narrow mercy—and of boundless hate. Killed senators by name, because he knew them; forgave by name, as he forgave Caesar, for amusement. He almost had it —mercy must go with killing to make a government, one won't work without the other; but not by name or face. People must believe that mercy's there for all, as well as punishment. . . . (*Caesar pauses. A long*

silence hanging from the sentence. Caesar still warming his fingers over the fire. He whispers) What
should I do?

HIRTIUS: The Senate thinks you want to hold them
in your hands, just so . . . (*Squeezes.*) . . . as Sulla
did, as God. I stand with Labienus' thinking. Seek
the hand of Pompey; then squeeze the Senate. A
little bit.

POLLIO: Oh, sir—I've been in Rome the years you've
been in Gaul. I go with Antony. Take the troops to
Rome and appeal your rights to the people in Assembly.

CAESAR: Appeal by force against the courts and law
and Senate? It will not stick, I say, unless one makes
one's self a God. I have the arms, but lack the law.
The law is what I need to make me consul—the
Senate to let me run, the people to vote me in; and
then, with *all* believing, we can change the rules.

HIRTIUS: I cannot understand.

CAESAR: (*Rising, infuriated*) If Hirtius cannot
understand, no one can. There is logic and there is
mercy; mercy must be impersonal as logic. They
must believe I will forgive. If they accept me, I forgive. Even the worst— Hirtius, I wish to send a
message. Take it down.

HIRTIUS: (*Acknowledging, taking his tablet*) Caesar. To whom?

CAESAR: To Cato. So Caesar speaks: (*Dictating and
pacing*) "Caesar Imperator to Cato sends Greetings:
Caesar's love of Rome is as great as Cato's; four centuries of the Republic look down on us. Cato is a man
of honor. I plead. Let me come to Rome and run for
consul. Make no traps, no ambushes. I offer in return:

every law obeyed, each dignity observed, no penal-
ties. Your word I trust. Give up your bitterness, and
I give up my armies. Let me speak to the people:
without a sword. Pledge me faith—and I return the
faith. No man marches. Hirtius bears this message.
He speaks for me. Tell him your thoughts."

HIRTIUS: (*Looking up from his pad, appalled*) I?
I go to Rome? My place is here with Caesar.

CAESAR: I need you more in Rome. Balbus goes to
Rome to bargain. They all know Balbus. But you
speak from closer to Caesar's inner thoughts—with
more authority. He to speak to Pompey and the senators. You to speak to Cato.

HIRTIUS: (*Assembling his tablet, stylus, and belong-
ings, knowing the answer before he asks his question*)
Now?

CAESAR: (*Watching him withdraw, compelling him
to withdraw*) This evening. (*As Hirtius exits, Caesar is alone with Pollio, who is standing, also about
to leave.*) Pollio?

POLLIO: Yes, sir.

CAESAR: What have you written?

POLLIO: Latin, sir.

CAESAR: No, not that. How does it sound to you?
What has Caesar said?

POLLIO: Caesar has given each his choice. Pompey.
Senate. Cato.

CAESAR: That's right. Well done. In Greek it would
sound like treachery. In Latin—that's the way things
are. Every man his choice.

POLLIO: Yes, sir.

CAESAR: And Caesar, too, must have a choice. Yes?

POLLIO: Yes, sir.

CAESAR: (*Sitting down, as if changing the subject*)
Do you understand about armies, Pollio?

POLLIO: Not much, sir.

CAESAR: Armies are a housekeeping business. Mostly
housekeeping. Almost entirely housekeeping. You
need the right number of men, there—(*Points*)—
with the right number of things in their hands. And
they should sleep well. And eat well. And then, a
little bit extra: they should believe it's worthwhile
dying. Soldiers used to die for Rome. My soldiers die
for Caesar.

POLLIO: Yes, sir.

CAESAR: How long does it take to move a legion
from Gaul to Rubicon, do you know?

POLLIO: I'm a headquarters correspondent, sir.

CAESAR: A matter of housekeeping again. It takes
four days' hard riding to reach Fabius' encampment
on the Rhone. December now. Winter camp is built.
Men in barracks, animals stabled with the Gauls.
Count five days for Fabius to strike and pack four
legions. Count eight days to supply food on line of
march for twenty thousand men. Normal marching
time—if all is ready in advance—twenty days—
forced march can make it ten days.

POLLIO: I'm not following you, sir.

CAESAR: (*Reaches to the mensa and draws close his
dice cup, which he rattles loudly.*) I mean—I, too,
must have a choice. (*Casts the dice, then gathers
them.*) Listen closely, Pollio, this is more than housekeeping, what I talk of now.

POLLIO: Sir . . . ? (*Pointing to himself—what else
is he doing but listening?*)

CAESAR: You too will take a trip. You leave tonight.

Back across the Alps to Gaul. To Fabius. As you go,
you pass instructions at the depots—to prepare food
on line of march. Tell Fabius: he will gather in the
animals. But quietly, as if it were a drill. With no
alarm. And then—(*Caesar clasps his hands together,
enjoying the thought artistically.*)—he must prepare
the signal flares.

POLLIO: Signal flares? What signal flares?

CAESAR: The Gallic legions know. And you will
learn. We learned the trick from Gauls. Like trousers.
Mattresses. Signal flares. If signals call, he must speed
to us as if speed alone would save the world. I want
his legions *here*, ten days from signal. If I call. As
Fabius breaks camp, he signals Trebonius in the north,
by flares. Who must be ready to split off two legions
from the Rhine guard and post them south to wait.
Don't write! (*Caesar takes tablet from Pollio's hand,
drops it in the fire, where it burns.*)

POLLIO: I wanted it exactly, sir.

CAESAR: The most important things in history are
what's not written. So this you carry in your head.
Tonight, you leave history for a week or two. You
act. You go. And no man knows you go. Not Antony, not Labienus, not Balbus. No man.

POLLIO: When, sir?

CAESAR: Tonight. After the banquet. You'll not be
missed. (*Picks up his dice, and rattles them.*) Other
men might think of this as treachery. You carry a
thought in Caesar's head. Only a vagrant thought for
now. All others now have choice. (*Spins the dice.*)
Caesar too deserves a choice. (*Gathers the dice.*) I've
offered choice. (*Spins the cup again.*) Let them
choose first. Then, next, I choose. But my choice is

easier if Fabius' legions are ten days' march away, rather than twenty days'. (*Picks up the dice.*) If they in Rome choose wisely, I've wasted a whole full week of Pollio's time. If they choose wrong . . . (*Shrugs his shoulders.*) Then maybe you will write of it. I give you leave—when I am dead, or triumphator.

CURTAIN

ACT TWO

SCENE ONE

TIME: Three weeks later, December 24.

PLACE: The same.

This scene must catch the Roman mood of carnival. The Romans stretched their law and discipline over a primitive world seething with savagery and superstition. The reactions in this scene, the music, the lighting must all suggest an underlying pagan madness. But there must be the suggestion of something more tender, too—for this is the seventh day of the revels of Saturnalia, a holiday of barbarian mercy and kindness, a time of giving gifts, the festival of short days and long nights which the Christians were later to appropriate and call Christmas.

Downstage, hunched over a stool at the left is Labienus, brooding. Upstage, on parapet, an incense pot is smoking; silver lamps flare.

POLLIO: (*As narrator, entering at right*) I went. I passed the messages. Then returned. Balbus, off to Rome, was back again; Hirtius, off to Rome, was back again. All assembled at headquarters because for us headquarters was our only home—and Saturnalia was time to be at home. Our legions used to celebrate the Saturnalia in December, from the Channel to the Gates of Hercules, from Tigris and Euphrates to the deserts of Africa. A time of gaiety and gifts, of singing and of kindness. You do the same in December, I understand. The nights are dark then, men think of God and home. So did we. (*Pollio retires upper right as Caesar enters.*)

(*Caesar enters right—in his brilliant new saffron gown of High Priest. He strides in lightly, twirls, pulls himself erect, then twirls again, as Labienus lifts his head, watches, and then Labienus' somber face breaks into a smile.*)

LABIENUS: (*Lifting his two arms above his head, in the greeting of respect*) Pontifex Maxime!

CAESAR: (*Gaily*) Like it?

LABIENUS: Splendid. I remember the first time you put one on—

CAESAR: —thirteen years ago—

LABIENUS: —and the old ladies and old men watching you at ceremony—

CAESAR: —all waiting for me to make a mistake. The music up the stairs. The white bull waiting for the knife. The lightning and the thunder at the altar—

LABIENUS: Remember how we fixed the thunder and the lightning—that Greek magician, what was his name?

CAESAR: (*Getting into the mood, now becomes mock-solemn, turns with back to audience, arms upturned, palms flat out from his shoulders in Roman supplication*) I forget . . . I even forget the chant . . . but it will be good to be in Rome again. . . .

(*Tries to chant . . . then sings out in clear loud voice.*)

LABIENUS: (*Admiring*) By Jupiter, you *are* Pontifex Maximus. . . . Nine years in Gaul and a man forgets. . . .

CAESAR: Of course I'm Pontifex Maximus. . . . I speak to Gods.

LABIENUS: I wish you'd talk to them now. We need a sign.

CAESAR: I'm talking to them. Watch. (*Ascends parapet, back to audience.*) Speak, Speak, Gods. Merry Saturn, speak to me. (*Silence. Caesar's voice becomes serious.*) Merry Saturn. Sweet God of earth and spring and sprouting. Speak. This is your holiday.

LABIENUS: (*As if talking about an insubordinate centurion, harshly, insistently*) He's angry. All the Gods are angry. But they *must* speak.

CAESAR: (*Slightly exasperated*) Saturn. It *is* your holiday. The Druids of Gaul hear their Gods talk. The Greeks hear Gods. Even the Jews can hear their God talk to them. . . . (*Lets his hands drop, then walks around the incense pot, studying the plume of smoke.*) That Greek magician could make the smoke blow any way I wanted it, gave me any omen I called for. Is this smoke blowing any particular way?

LABIENUS: (*Studying the smoke*) Goes straight up. I wish it would blow one way or the other— either we go to Rome, or we don't. Sitting here like this gets us nowhere.

CAESAR: (*Puts his hands on hips, as if remonstrating, turns face up to talk to Saturn.*) I am Pontifex Maximus and you are Saturn. We have a contract. If you are a God, Saturn, you are God on this side of the Rubicon as well as the other. (*Studies the smoke. Then, in a burst of real anger*) Which way—show me! There is Italy. There the mountains. Which way? (*Smoke continues to rise straight up.*) Speak. Blow. Give me an omen. This is your day to speak.

(*Absolute silence. Labienus shakes his head gloomily, and then Caesar resumes his rigid upright posture, hands upraised, palms upturned.*)

(*The silence is suddenly broken by a noise. Below, from the courtyard beneath the parapet, a burst of sounds —drunken voices, song, loud howling, laughter, revelry, which rises to disturb.*)

CAESAR: (*Drops his hands, goes to the parapet, shouts*) Quiet! Quiet! Stop it! (*The noise gradually subsides, and Caesar strides to the wings and calls.*) Commander of the Guard! Commander! Ho!

COMMANDER: (*Following Caesar in immediately*) Imperator!

CAESAR: Commander—what in Hades is going on down there?

COMMANDER: Spirit of Saturnalia, sir. You know how troops get, sir—been in barracks for weeks, all rested and fat, full of juice, sir. No women, lots of drink.

CAESAR: Well, why down there in headquarters courtyard?

COMMANDER: They came to borrow a few Gauls from the dungeons, sir.

CAESAR: Borrow a few Gauls!!!!????

COMMANDER: They won't hurt them, sir. The captives are in chains. Can't get away.

CAESAR: But those Gauls are for the triumph parade

in Rome—for ceremony! Not slave Gauls. We have
to march them through the Forum!

LABIENUS: (*Intervening, confessing*) I said it
would be all right, Imperator, if they don't bruise
them.

CAESAR: You said—what?!

LABIENUS: (*Doggedly*) I gave them leave. It's the
last night of Saturnalia. They finished gift-giving
several days ago. They're homesick. And there's been
no banquet for the slaves.

CAESAR: But there are no slaves here.

LABIENUS: It's just the ceremonies . . . the ceremonies. . . . We have no omens, the Gods are angry.
You're Pontifex Maximus. The Saturnalia calls for
banquets for the slaves—

CAESAR: I know, I know—and bathing slaves, and
crowning them, and oiling them, and serving them.
And it would please you if we found slaves so we
could serve them.

LABIENUS: So, I said—let the troops use the Gauls
as slaves, this night, just once.

CAESAR: (*Cocking his head to one side, then,
grandly*) Well . . . why not? But do it right. I'll
wash a slave and oil him, too, myself. . . . High
Priest always tends a slave on Saturnalia. . . .
Where's Vercingetorix!

LABIENUS: Vercingetorix? In the dungeons, with
his Gauls.

CAESAR: I haven't seen him since he surrendered at
Alesia. . . . Bring him up.

LABIENUS: Here?

CAESAR: Fetch him. (*To the Commander of the
Guard*) Bring him here at once.

(*Commander exits.*)

LABIENUS: But why Vercingetorix?

CAESAR: Vercingetorix will act as my slave. If the Gods need ceremonies before they give us signs, we'll do it right. I have given my gifts. Performed the ceremonies. Implored. And cannot get a sign from Saturn. So—I will tend a slave—myself. Vercingetorix, chief slave. Is he well?

LABIENUS: They feed him well. Eats enough for two men. Growls when they talk to him. Has learned some Latin in the dungeon. . . .

CAESAR: Too bad. He'll never get a chance to use it. I liked him, though. Too bad he has to die.

LABIENUS: A savage. If we had lost at Alesia, he would have slaved or killed us every one—and we let his people go.

CAESAR: Yes. Yes . . . but to die in battle's one thing. To die by strangling in the pit's another. He had a dignity . . . even when he surrendered, he had his dignity. It's easier dying than to lose your dignity. . . .

(*As Caesar speaks, enter Vercingetorix. He is a huge man. Blond. Tumbling blond curls, tumbling long blond mustaches. He carries himself proudly—but even in his filth, he is menacing. He is dressed in dirty breeches and a woolen tunic. Ankle chains of iron bind his feet. He hobbles. His hands, in front of him, are locked in a wooden bar so that he can move them within the stock locks—but not free them. He is prodded out on to stage by two legionaries followed by the Commander, and he blinks. Lights are up, high, as he enters.*)

CAESAR: Sit him down. (*They pull out a stool and*

thrust it under Vercingetorix.) Now—leave us. (*To Labienus*) Have them send us meats—and the washing bowl.

(*Exit soldiers. Exit Labienus. Soldiers will return shortly with the meats and footbowl, then leave.*)

(*Vercingetorix slowly lifts his shaggy head and, with a majestic slow quality, turns to peer about the stage from side to side, returning finally to fix his gaze on Caesar.*)

VERCINGETORIX: Vercingetorix sees Caesar.

CAESAR: (*Courteously, as if returning a bow*)   Caesar sees Vercingetorix.

(*They stare at each other.*)

VERCINGETORIX: Caesar has come back from Gaul.

CAESAR: You see me here. I came some days ago.

VERCINGETORIX: I know. They told me in the dungeon. In Gaul—is quiet?

CAESAR: Very quiet. All peaceful. We are friends now.

VERCINGETORIX: Then they have forgotten Vercingetorix.

CAESAR: No. Not yet. But they will. And then remember him again—much later.

VERCINGETORIX: What will you do with Gaul?

CAESAR: The Senate and People—in Rome they will decide.

VERCINGETORIX: (*Shaking his shaggy head*) Caesar will decide. I know.

CAESAR: How so?

VERCINGETORIX: The leader decides. One man says. I know. I was leader. But they did not understand. Do your people understand?

CAESAR: (*Ruefully*) Not yet.

VERCINGETORIX: (*Smiling, nodding*) And you must make them understand. This is hard. Very hard. I do not have this problem, now— (*Vercingetorix stops, puzzled, as a huge bowl of cold meats is brought in. They place it before him.*)

CAESAR: (*Observing his puzzlement, smiling*) Eat.

VERCINGETORIX: Caesar eats with Vercingetorix?

CAESAR: This is Saturn's feast—fresh meat. Wine? Or mead if you want it? I am not hungry, so I do not eat. Tonight I act as priest. I wear these robes for Saturn.

VERCINGETORIX: (*Munching as he talks, with gusto*) So. I did not know you were a priest. I saw you only in the battle.

CAESAR: In battle, when I am imperator, I wear scarlet. For blood. So troops can follow. But I am a priest, too—the Great Priest of Rome.

VERCINGETORIX: Ah, so. Roman priests wear yellow, and go to battle? Our priests wear blue. They do not go to battle, they only pray. That is how you win?—your Gods go with you?

CAESAR: No. Our Gods stay in Rome. They tell the people what to do. The people send out legions to make war.

VERCINGETORIX: How?

CAESAR: The people gather in the Forum. Then, when the Gods give signs that they may talk, they make the laws, and speak for God. All talk until they agree to make a law.

VERCINGETORIX: (*Unbelieving*) The *people* make the law?

CAESAR: Oh, we *say* they do. Whatever's done in

Rome, we say the people do it, or we say we do it *for* the people.

VERCINGETORIX: *Very* dangerous.

CAESAR: No. Very useful. You see, we let the people vote. . . .

VERCINGETORIX: Vote?! All the people—vote?

CAESAR: (*Continuing*) Then if they *vote* to go to war, they all must fight, they answer muster.

VERCINGETORIX: In Gaul, much simpler.

CAESAR: How do you do it?

VERCINGETORIX: Princes call assembly when they want to go to war. They beat the drums, they ring the gongs. All men come running to muster place. Last man who comes running to muster place —we kill him. That way muster is fast.

CAESAR: (*Laughing*) Good idea. But not in Rome. The Gods would not approve.

VERCINGETORIX: Where do your Gods do this? Where do they live?

CAESAR: Above the Hill in Rome. The sky there is full of Gods. More every year.

VERCINGETORIX: (*They are now engaged in the shop talk of leaders.*) Our Gods live in trees. In rivers. In stones. Our Gods are everywhere. But the Gods talk only to Druids. The Druids tell the princes, and then, together, princes and Druids decide. The people do *not* talk. The Druids say when war must come, but they must not go to battle, see a sword, fight in war.

CAESAR: (*Pulling over his own stool, sits near Vercingetorix*) Very interesting. The Druids do not fight, they only say when to kill.

VERCINGETORIX: And whom to kill. Only the

Druids know what Gods want. When a man dies, Gods tell Druids who killed him. Sometimes maybe it is his brother. Or his wife. Druids know—they say.

CAESAR: Then what happens?

VERCINGETORIX: Then they say: burn the brother; maybe burn his wife. Druids know why famine comes. Then they say how many people the Gods want burned.

CAESAR: How do they choose the men they burn?

VERCINGETORIX: The Druids say to burn, then the princes choose. Criminals. Thieves. If all criminals and thieves are burned up—they burn common people. The prince says which of his people should be burned.

CAESAR: The prince can choose?

VERCINGETORIX: Every man has a prince to protect him. If the prince protects a people's life, then he can give it away, too? Not right?

CAESAR: Without a trial?

VERCINGETORIX: We are free people. If the people do not like their lords, they can run away. But then who would protect them? Anyway—if they die, they will live later. If innocent, they will be born again as prince, or lark, or oak. If guilty, they will live again as snake, or stone, or dog.

CAESAR: When a Roman dies, he does not live again. He is very dead. We kill few citizens. We exile them for crimes—and even then it cannot be done without a trial.

VERCINGETORIX: Even if the Gods speak clearly —even then a trial?

CAESAR: Roman Gods do not speak clearly. They give signs. When the signs are read—then men who know the signs can speak for Gods.

VERCINGETORIX: (*Shaking his head*) Difficult. Difficult for you. How do you read the signs?

CAESAR: Usually we use a sheep; we cut it open and read its gut; or a chicken.

VERCINGETORIX: A chicken?

CAESAR: A chicken.

VERCINGETORIX: (*Laughing out loud*) Chicken! Our Gods want man. We stretch a *man* out on the rocks; the Druids pray. They they rip his belly open and watch the blood flow; while his guts are warm and moving, they pull them out and read God's will. Chickens!

CAESAR: (*Laughing too*) Chickens. And the way birds fly. Crows. Eagles. Sparrows. And the way lightning goes. The augurs tell us what the signs mean. If the signs are right and give them leave, then the people speak for God, choosing leaders, consuls, tribunes; voting judges, voting laws. You see—the people must be flattered to believe that they voice the will of God. If they believe . . . that way all our tribes and people are bound as one—you see?

VERCINGETORIX: No. We have tribes, too—Arverni, Aedui, Remi, Sequani, Suessoni. No tribe accepts the leaders of another tribe. I tried to make all tribes be one. (*Then, a thought striking him, puzzled*) But Rome is not one, either. Caesar has enemies in Rome. I know.

CAESAR: Yes. I want to make the whole world one. Some in Rome disagree.

VERCINGETORIX: To make the whole world one . . . *very* hard. One God for all the world? They are right who disagree.

CAESAR: I have contracts. With the law. With the Gods. With the soldiers. Even with your Gauls. This is what makes it hard.

VERCINGETORIX: With Gauls? Which Gauls?

CAESAR: All Gauls. Even your tribe. I set your Arverni free after Alesia—because I promised Vercingetorix, if he surrendered, his Arverni would be free, not slaves.

VERCINGETORIX: But I must die?

CAESAR: Why . . . yes. You had a treaty with Rome. When you broke the treaty, you broke a law. Vercingetorix led his tribe to break the treaty. Someone must pay. Gauls must know they cannot break Rome's laws.

VERCINGETORIX: But it was a *Roman* law, not a Gallic law I broke. Our Gods said we must be free again. The Druids said it was their will. They told me so.

CAESAR: Then the Gallic Gods will make you live again. Come. You have eaten. Now I will care for you.

VERCINGETORIX: (*Sullenly*) Because your Gods say so?

CAESAR: Because Saturn wishes kindness done on his festival to the slaves. (*Approaching Vercingetorix, Caesar wipes his face with a wet cloth from a steaming bowl.*)

VERCINGETORIX: Slave?

(*Caesar is very gentle as he salves and wipes Vercingetorix' mouth.*)

VERCINGETORIX: I am not slave. I am Vercingetorix. Captive but free!

CAESAR: (*Stooping beneath Vercingetorix' hands*)

I wash your feet. This is Saturn's feast of kindness to
the slaves.

VERCINGETORIX: (*Anger rising; panic and anger
both in his voice*) No! Do not touch my feet! Slaves
have no afterlife. Slaves die dead! They become
stones! Kill Vercingetorix! Do not touch me as a
slave!

CAESAR: We all die dead. It is Caesar himself who
tends you—

(*The following is a scene for the actors' and director's
imagination: Caesar bends, but he is stopped in mid-
sentence as Vercingetorix plunges manacled hands
down to Caesar's throat. He grabs and throttles. Basin
spills. Stool tumbles. The huge Vercingetorix has
Caesar on the ground. They wrestle—until, with a
violent wrench, Caesar pulls loose from the hobbled
Vercingetorix, leaving his yellow priestly gown torn
in Vercingetorix' clutch. Vercingetorix attempts to
follow, trips on his ankle chain. Caesar kneels on Vercingetorix' back, twists the yellow hair up, holds the
dagger to throat. Caesar pants for a moment.*)

CAESAR: (*Shouting, kneeling in victory over Vercingetorix*) Guard! Commander of the Guard!
(*Stooping, panting over Vercingetorix*) I gave you
back ten thousand lives at Alesia—all your Arverni
free. That was what you said—your life for theirs.
Whoever breaks the law of Rome must die.

VERCINGETORIX: Vercingetorix surrendered to
be killed—not to be a slave. No foot-washing by a
chicken-watcher. A bargain—

CAESAR: (*Still panting*) As you will. I will not
wash your feet. But you are captive still, who broke
a law. Not slave—but will be dead, no less. (*Re-

leasing grip on head, letting him rise)
(*Soldiers enter with Commander.*)

COMMANDER. (*Seeing Caesar stripped of his robe*) Imperator! (*Pulling out sword, advancing on Vercingetorix*) Sir—that bastard's dangerous. (*To soldiers*) Grab him!

(*Enter Labienus.*)

LABIENUS: (*Taking in scene*) What happened? Caesar? (*To Vercingetorix*) You mother-loving, jumping, blue-balled, breech-bound bastard—in our dungeon—

CAESAR: (*Interrupting*) Do not harm him. Take him away. He did not want his feet washed. Does not want to be a slave—even at Saturnalia. (*As they are about to take Vercingetorix*) Oh—and Commander? Bathe him! He smells bad. A Roman bath. (*To Vercingetorix*) A free man's bath. I give my word.

(*Exit guard, Commander and Vercingetorix.*)

CAESAR: (*To Labienus*) He is young. And very strong.

LABIENUS: I will never understand Caesar. A Roman of fifty-two wrestling with a Gaul of thirty. What happened? If I only knew what you were thinking.

CAESAR: That the Gauls will make good citizens. (*Aware suddenly that he is in underclothes*) And there is something to be said for Gallic breeches after all. Easier to wrestle in. (*Stoops to pick up saffron High Priest's robe.*) Here, take this. I must go and change. (*Caesar begins to exit right, but mounts to look at incense pot.*) So much for ceremony. Saturn has no message for us this season. No omen. What we must decide, we must decide ourselves. Are Curio and Balbus rested from their journey up from Rome?

LABIENUS: All here.

CAESAR: Call them. Call the evening conference. (*Snuffs out torches with silver snuffing cup.*) I'll be ready as soon as I change. See the troops return the Gauls to the dungeons. At once. (*Snuffs out the incense pot. Stands for a moment in priestly posture, arms upraised, palms upturned. Gazes at the sky.*) Farewell, Merry Saturn.

(*Caesar leaves, Labienus stares after him.*)

CURTAIN

SCENE TWO

T I M E :   Fifteen minutes later.
P L A C E :   The same.
Present: Labienus, Hirtius, Balbus, Pollio, all of whom
we have met before. Plus a newcomer: Curio, ex-
tribune, just up from Rome, where Antony has replaced him in office on December 10.

P O L L I O :   (*As narrator*) Thus, the last day of Saturnalia. No word, no sign from on high, the calendar
racing on to month's end, when on the first of January the two incoming consuls, taking office, always
state their program to the Senate in the Hall of Jupiter.
The *nobiles* had won both consulships. Lentulus Crus,
a weakling—he would echo other men. But also Gaius
Marcellus, finest blood in Rome. Three years running
now, a Marcellus has been elected consul—two broth-
ers, a cousin. Their first names mean so little—but the
family name! Ancestral honors running back to Rom-
ulus himself, the death masks in their courtyard a
museum of every hero back to Carthage and beyond.
Never mind.

This new Marcellus, Gaius, would speak within the
week and tell the Senate of his course. Marcellus,
pushed about himself—by Cato and the faction, by
Pompey and his troops, by mobs, by other men's ambitions. All hating each other; but fearing Caesar
more.

One week more before they froze on policy.

They in Rome—and we so near, so far away.

(*Curtain parts as the conference waits for Caesar. All
chatting.*)

LABIENUS: . . . knee in his back, I tell you. Caesar
on top, his dagger in the animal's throat. Wouldn't
call for help until he had him down, and the animal
might have killed him.

POLLIO: (*Busy taking notes, looks up*)   If Vercingetorix had killed him, they would have made a God of
Caesar—died on Saturnalia, doing mercy after triumph.

HIRTIUS: One way or another, Caesar dead will be
a God. But too many in Rome want him dead now.
He is safer here among the people of Po valley than
he'll be in Rome.

LABIENUS: I tell you, the Gods are angry with us.
We prayed together. I watched him. Saturn would
not give a sign, and he Pontifex Maximus himself. I
do not like it, I tell you, I do not like it. . . . Nothing fits together. It does not fit. . . .

(*Enter Caesar, as Labienus talks. All rise, salute. But Caesar is brisk and businesslike.*)

CAESAR: What does not fit? (*Looks around.*) Sit.
What does not fit?

LABIENUS: Nothing fits. The Gods are angry. The
Senate torn. Pompey cold.

CAESAR: What news from Rome? What messengers today? Curio—you're freshest up from Rome, how do you read it now?

CURIO: (*He is a tall, lean, sallow type. Not a soldier, a politician—for the past year he has been Caesar's paid agent, as tribune, on the Senate floor. A cold man*) The evening couriers have come—but no news. We can't expect hard news for days. All wait for the opening of the Senate, so what happens now is happening secretly. In gossip and at banquets. At dinner parties where they plot. In Pompey's mansion. Rome's a-buzz. Or in Cato's villa . . .

CAESAR: But what does Cato want? There must be something that will satisfy him. . . . Hirtius, you spoke to him.

HIRTIUS: I tried and tried again. He wants you small, because he wants Rome small. Repeats himself and then repeats himself, like a priest chanting in a temple. Caesar must submit to law, must put down arms when law requires, give up command, return to Rome and face his peers. . . .

LABIENUS: I say: ignore him. Cato is one man only, no army, never fought in battle.

CURIO: He will not be ignored. Cato is an idea. He speaks of law; and the Senate thinks of spoils and cheers him on. Cato says: the wars are over, emergency passed, extraordinary commands like Caesar's should end. The Senate listens, applauds, each family of *nobiles* thinking how to share out Caesar's conquests.

BALBUS: In every temple courtyard, in every boudoir where the ladies gossip, they carve the world: Domitius Ahenobarbus to have Gaul; the Scipios to have Syria; Faustus Sulla, Mauretania.

LABIENUS: Talk. Talk. Talk. What the legions won
is not for politicians to give away. Talk. Ignore them.
Get to Pompey, he's a soldier. His troops will press
upon the Senate more than Cato's speeches.

BALBUS: Get to Pompey, get to Pompey . . . and
so I got to Pompey, who tells me he is Pompey, which
I knew. The faction flatters him. Even Cato flatters
him. He swells. By leave of Senate, he drills recruits.
He holds two legions, at Capua—all in obedience to
the Senate, he says to me. He wobbles now and then,
speaks of old friendship, but urges Caesar, too, obey
the Senate and the laws it makes.

CAESAR: (*Who has now begun, idly, to rattle his
dice, and slowly begins to cast them*)   It does fit, it
does fit. All fits together. But *their* way, not ours.
Pompey has the troops, the Senate has the law. Our
troops are better, our voters more. Only our troops
are here, our voters far from Rome. (*Casts his dice.*)
Curio? Curio, you are silent. What reading do you
make of it?

CURIO: I do not like to read it. Until last fortnight,
I bore the tribune's rods in Rome. Then came here.
And slept. Slept the night and day, and night and day
again. No shrieking in my ears. I woke and walked
Ravenna's marketplace. And found I'd left my dag-
ger behind—but did not feel afraid. Safer here with
Caesar in Ravenna's streets than in Rome, as tribune.

CAESAR: (*Rattling dice again*)   And yet, somehow
it must be made to fit.

CURIO: Caesar has been away. In the city, the mobs,
ours and theirs, both monsters. North of Rome—
some with the Senate, some with us. The more north,

the more with us. Here in the valley—all freeholders, all knights, all farmers, solidly with us. But they can't get to Rome to vote—and there you have it.

CAESAR: (*Lets dice roll.*) See. How clear it is. We must get to vote. And thus to get to vote we must yield something—to Pompey or to Senate. And must do it now. Another week will see them frozen together. When Senate opens, it will be too late.

HIRTIUS: What can we give we have not already offered?

CAESAR: More. Up to now we have explored. Now we beg. To satisfy the Senate—I give up Gaul-Beyond-the-Alps. Let them divide it by their greed until we make new laws. The Senate voted me command of Gaul-Beyond-the-Alps; I give it back at their request. But Gaul-Within-the-Alps, this valley, is ours by people's vote. This I hold by people's vote until Assembly gathers once again. . . . Then, Pompey—

BALBUS: Pompey also wants you small, O Caesar.

HIRTIUS: Not like Cato. Cato wants you small to keep Rome small. Pompey wants you small to make himself great.

CAESAR: I can crouch until the voters vote. To satisfy Pompey's dignity, I will cut my legions. By three, four, five, however many he wants. He has two in Italy. I will hold two here in the valley.

LABIENUS: That's it. There's dignity enough to share. But with Pompey, not the Senate; the legions are the state in arms, are Rome—

CURIO: No—and no—and no. You both have been away. The more Caesar offers, the more they'll think him weak. They will not bargain until they know that Caesar means to use his strength—or see it glint.

LABIENUS: You draw our sword to see it glint?
Against Pompey? And how does it get back into the
scabbard? Roman legion must not fight Roman legion.

CAESAR: Labienus, my man of war, wants peace. But
Curio, my man of politics, wants just a glint of steel,
a taste of force?

CURIO: Just a taste. The sound of horns.

BALBUS: The sound of horns, yes. Or a parade. Just
one of Caesar's legions in parade. We bring Vercingetorix to strangle him in the pit. The mobs would
howl, to see Vercingetorix in his cage. Once there—
we stay to vote.

LABIENUS: (*Contemptuously*) Parades! Even if
they agreed . . . you talk as if mountains, miles, distances were not there. The Senate meets next week.
Debates another week. Two weeks for us to act. And
half our legions are watching Germans on the Rhine,
two months' march from here. Half along the Rhone
—four weeks to break camp and move the fastest of
them here—

CAESAR: No . . . ten days only and we have two
legions here. Ten more days, all four from the Rhone.

LABIENUS: How, Caesar, how? You talk to city
politicians like a city-soldier who never had to break
a camp and set it on the march.

CAESAR: If we light the signal fires here, this night—
Fabius marches in the morning.

CURIO: Caesar—light the signals. This is the only language the Senate understands.

LABIENUS: Impossible. Explain, Caesar, or let me
explain. To prepare a winter march, animals must be

drawn in. Food stocked. Fabius must be given notice. Weeks must pass. While Pompey also moves his legions north.

CAESAR: Fabius is already packed, Labienus. Food and stores already in stock on line of march. Signal fires, Gallic-style, from hill to hill already on standby.

LABIENUS: (*Separating himself from the group, stalking slowly across stage, then turning at far right like a prosecutor*) By whose orders? I am Caesar's legate, chief-of-staff.

CAESAR: By Caesar's orders.

LABIENUS: When?

CAESAR: Three weeks ago.

LABIENUS: And I was not informed? No one was informed? Then all your messengers to Rome were liars? Balbus a liar, Curio a liar, Hirtius a liar—Labienus a liar? I, who wrote to Pompey we have not moved a man? Pompey, who trusts me still—

CAESAR: (*Interrupting, curtly*) By whose authority did you write to Pompey?

LABIENUS: I wrote as Labienus, your chief-of-staff and Pompey's old lieutenant. I wrote for peace. And now I am a liar—all of us liars. Or—or do all of you know, Curio, Hirtius, Balbus, Pollio, even Antony— knowing liars! And only Labienus a fool, a witless liar, a battle-hack trusted only to stand and fight. Caesar did not trust me.

CAESAR: No man has moved—so no man is a liar. And no one knew but Pollio, who took my message. It is only a thought in my mind—not a deed. If deeds must come, thoughts must precede them. No single cohort moves until I raise a signal. And then, Labienus, my chief-of-staff, gives the signal.

LABIENUS: I give no signal to march on Rome. . . .
(*Sits on stool, facing audience, head down, stunned.*)
Caesar did not trust me. Whom does Caesar trust if
not Labienus?

(*Caesar now crosses to far left, where Labienus is sitting.
As Labienus leans forward, Caesar stands behind him,
occasionally with hand on shoulder, affectionately;
occasionally aloof and cold, pleading for understanding all the while.*)

CAESAR: I not trust Labienus? Our first action against
Helvetians nine years ago—who held them off, when
I raced back for reinforcements? When we crossed
the Rhine—who led the vanguard? When I crossed
to England and left the legions behind—whom did I
trust? Who commanded all Gaul in my name?

LABIENUS: (*Grudgingly*) I.

CAESAR: I not trust Labienus? When all Gaul rose
two years ago, and I came across the Alps in winter
snow—who held it firm until I came? Who held the
angle of the hill above Alesia through the siege?

LABIENUS: (*Still grudgingly, yet stirred*) I.

CAESAR: (*Runs his hand down Labienus' forearm,
picks it up, examines the inner elbow*) And here, all
healed, the scar. Chief-of-staff dueling with a Gallic
bladesman. Trying to make Imperator proud of him
as if he were a centurion. Caesar not trust Labienus?
(*Caesar changes mood, becomes stern.*) I do not mis-
trust Labienus because he wrote to Pompey—

LABIENUS: I did it for *you*. To *help* you. Pompey
trusts me. I served as staff lieutenant in his pirate
wars.

CAESAR: You wrote without telling me. Yet I understand. *I* am not angry. It was a thought in your mind. Now *you* are angry because I do not tell you what is only thinking in my mind.

LABIENUS: It is different. Caesar does not have to understand Labienus. Labienus *has* to understand Caesar—because he is Caesar.

CAESAR: What is there to understand? I do not want to fight. Nor do I want to strike. Yet Rome is mine as much as theirs. I offer peace, I bring it victory. I have the right to stand for consul. They have no right to strip me of this right, to stand me up for trial. I am Caesar! I have a dignity. Easier give my life in battle than let them take my dignity away. . . .

LABIENUS: (*Under stress*)   I am afraid, I am afraid.

CAESAR: Of what?

LABIENUS: Of what is in your mind.

CAESAR: What would you have me do?

LABIENUS: Roman legion must not fight Roman legion. Do not let them turn Pompey to fight you. Make peace with Pompey—the eagles must not clash—

CAESAR: But I have tried, Labienus. I offer Pompey equal dignity. I have sent messengers to plead with him.

LABIENUS: You sent Balbus—a Spanish alien to talk to him.

CAESAR: What would you have me do? Walk the road in person? Invite him to conspire with me, to purge the Senate by sword until we two, alone, divide the world? Rome is more than what two generals decide. . . .

LABIENUS: (*Rising*)   More than what one general decides, either. For fifteen years, from Forum to the

forests of Germany, I have followed the fantasies you
dream—but now I cannot understand your dreams.

CAESAR: These are not fantasies I dream. But night-
mares. You wish to be consul. So do I. We plan to
run together next year as partners in the Fifth Month
elections. Because we know what must be done. Because what we have done these years beyond the
Alps has swollen Rome so large it now must change.
But what if they take our dignity, our lives, from us
before we wear the consul's robes—what then?

CURIO: Rome will not change unless Caesar acts. No
law, no Senate resolution, no court is firm. I come
here from a year in office, I tell you Rome is Rome
no longer unless Caesar acts.

LABIENUS: (*Turning on Curio*) Who are you to
say when Caesar acts? Who are you to speak for
legions you never saw and never marched with?

CAESAR: He speaks with my leave, Labienus. He
comes from Rome and politics.

LABIENUS: (*Beginning to rage—turning on all of
them*) A city politician! An alien! A scribbling boy!
A secretary on horseback! All have the right to
speak? All have the right to counsel on what the legions do? Where they go? Whom they kill?

CAESAR: These are my men. They bring me facts.
All here are equal.

LABIENUS: (*Scornfully*) All equal in your presence. This is Caesar's court, not Caesar's camp—
courtiers, twisting and luring Caesar to their own
ambitions—

CAESAR: Labienus, guard yourself—I am Caesar,
still.

LABIENUS: (*Furiously*) And I am Caesar's chief-

of-staff, runningmate for consulship next year. I am
not a wooden blade to be drawn at will when other
men have Caesar's ear. I am not a fool behind whose
back a little boy is sent to mobilize my legions on the
Rhone—

CAESAR:　Not your legions, Labienus—Caesar's legions!

LABIENUS:　Rome's legions! Rome's legions drawn
to fight with other Roman legions!

CAESAR:　Labienus, go! Go before you say too much
and cannot draw it back. Go. Now. And I will come
to you to talk alone. (*Labienus draws himself erect,
controlling himself as he is dismissed. Caesar continues*) Go. And think a little while. No legion
marches. No signal fires are lit until the Gods speak
clear. I, too, must think. And then if signal fires are
lit, the order passes through my chief-of-staff.

LABIENUS:　(*Sullenly*)　I do not want to march on
Rome. I leave you with your court. I go.

(*Exit Labienus. All watch him go, silently.*)

HIRTIUS:　(*Fussily, tentatively*)　He must be very
angry . . . to break the rules and speak like that . . .

CAESAR:　There are no rules in friendship. And we've
been friends. And he's been friends with Pompey,
too. He fought with Pompey in the pirate wars when
he was young—furrowing the great seas, hunting the
high-peaked prows, sweeping the waves. He still
talks of it as any junior officer talks about his first
campaign, his first commander. The memory glows—
the silver sails, the golden oars, the peace they made,
his first renown. He remembers Pompey from afar—
the hero-leader, and he a boy. Labienus joined me as
a man, a partner; has seen me weep, has watched me

bleed; he knows my faults—and thinks me weak.

CURIO: Weak?

POLLIO: Weak? Caesar weak?

CAESAR: Weak . . . to bargain with the men of politics. Rome, to him, is armies; the sacrament and oath that binds the men in arms; all else is decoration. Honors for him are earned in battle; of these the greatest is the consulship for which we stand together. To beg or bargain for the honor is beneath contempt —thus he despises politicians. To snatch the consulship by force of arms—is profanation. This leaves him with no way but Pompey—a soldier like ourselves, a general of the armies.

POLLIO: But other generals have marched on Rome and seized the consulship before.

CAESAR: Sulla did—and now for thirty years Rome has been recovering from the shock. It will not stand a second shock—there Labienus is right.

HIRTIUS: I was there when Sulla entered through the Martian Gate. . . . He broke the rules.

CAESAR: He broke the faith. I was eighteen—and pledged to be a priest, *flamen dialis*, an acolyte in Jupiter's Temple, a boy brought up by women, mother, sisters, aunts, when my father died. (*Pollio furtively starts scribbling, and Caesar turns on him.*) Women who still believed. When women lose religion, all faith is lost. To them, to me, the Gods' will was clear, Rome's laws were Gods', her triumphs theirs. And thus, the ancient rule: no legions enter Rome in drill formation except by invitation of the Senate for the ceremonial parade to show their triumph to the Gods.

Then, Sulla.

Sulla!

He brought his legions *in!* Into the city. The legionaries came marching in . . . to fight. They were
citizens like us. But, bound together in the legion,
they terrified me—their horns calling and screaming,
their eagles dancing. This was sacrilege. Women and
children ran. And I, I who meant to be a priest,
watched and waited for the Gods to strike him dead.

POLLIO: What happened?

CAESAR: Then nothing happened.

Nothing.

They killed.

They held the city in terror. Take them apart, pull
down banners, horns, eagles, strip their armor—and
they were single men, frail, like us. They believed in
Sulla, not Gods—or believed in Sulla because he said
he spoke for the Gods. Take Sulla from them, the
glue that bound them, and they were nothing. What
few are left of them today—beggars in the Forum
now, toothless veterans of Asian wars; half-blind,
homeless, landless scum, their votes for sale, too old
to fight, too tired for honor. Yet they as legions held
Rome; and Rome held the world. Nor would the
Gods step in to stay them once Sulla told them: kill.
Pollio, there's much to learn from Sulla.

POLLIO: Sir . . . what?

CAESAR: Oh, many, many lessons—one of which is
that Gods bow to the legions, not legions to the Gods.

CURIO: Caesar . . . sir . . . one caution: we speak
in Caesar's quarters, here. But this is what they wish
to make you say aloud, in Rome.

CAESAR: What do they wish to make me say?

CURIO: That Caesar has no faith in the Gods, repudiates them.

CAESAR: Come now, Curio. I am High Priest. Conqueror of Gaul. Who can make me say so? How? Where? When?

CURIO: At trial.

CAESAR: For what?

CURIO: For sacrilege. This is Cato's plan, I tell you. I come from Rome. This is why they plan to strip you of the scarlet cloak now; then summon you to Rome *before* elections, then stand Caesar up for trial—for sacrilege.

CAESAR: But I have been in Gaul nine years . . . the Gods have smiled on me.

CURIO: And by the laws just passed, indictments run back twenty years. Thus all of Caesar's acts as consul ten years ago are called in question—and Bibulus will testify, it is planned.

CAESAR: Old Bibulus, co-consul in my term, victory of the balanced ticket, he, conservative, and I a *popularis.* (*Caesar hunches over like a stiff arthritic and mimics the absent Bibulus, a high-pitched, cranky-voiced old man.*) "Be careful, Caesar. Beware, Caesar. The omens are wrong, Caesar. The Gods will not permit Assembly to vote today, Caesar. Lightning from the left, Caesar—the Gods forbid a vote today." . . . Oh, nonsense, Curio, nonsense.

BALBUS: Yes, Caesar. Nonsense, Caesar. Nonsense, of course, nonsense. But Curio is right, too. If they can make you say nonsense in public—

CAESAR: But everyone *knows* it is nonsense. Are we Gauls, to be ruled by superstition? I had things to do.

I observed the ceremonies. Ceremonies are useful. No one is more careful than I of ceremony. I put the chickens out before each Assembly. They hopped the way they should, to left or right, they pecked or cast out grain to give the omens. I had those chickens trained myself.

CURIO: Do not say that, Caesar. The College of Augurs will testify against you.

CAESAR: The College of Augurs? Every consul finds an augur to tell him what he wants, just as Gauls have Druids to tell them what they want. Have you ever heard the augurs argue about lightning? I sat with them when I was consul. Lightning is the message of the Gods, they say. But who can read it? Lightning over left shoulder before noon—bad? Lightning over right shoulder before noon—good? Lightning behind the clouds—good or bad? Do the Gods want the people to talk or not? And one augur sees lightning, the other sees nothing. This is not the way the Gods talk—if they talk at all. I could not wait for them to work out riddles, decide which day, which hour the people might gather and vote on laws. The laws I passed as consul nine years ago, I *had* to pass. And must pass other laws next year if Rome is to stay Rome. Gods silent, or Gods speaking.

CURIO: This is why they are afraid. This is what they plan to make you say.

CAESAR: (*Pacing now, in fury*) Curio. I have been High Priest now for fourteen years. I stand with legions at my back. If they, the Gods, had messages to give, they would give messages to *me*. Directly. Not through chickens, eagles, lightning, augurs. I plead with them. (*Turning back to audience, palms upward in priestly stance, but rigid, not as a supplicant*) I, Caesar, plead. I *need* to know. (*Silence as they watch him.*) They will not speak.

BALBUS: (*Repeating, as usual*) They will not speak. But you must not say so, Caesar.

CAESAR: They will not speak, I say, they will not speak. They *never* speak.

POLLIO: (*Still writing in his tablet*) Sir—not ever?

CAESAR: Put away your tablet.
Not ever. Not ever. Sometimes when I thought I heard them speak, it was only myself, my own voice talking to me, saying what I would say if I were God.

CURIO: What does it say, the voice?

CAESAR: It says: Save Rome. It says: Rome is not a city, it is the world. It says: Every man must vote who is a citizen. Within the city or beyond its walls. It says: The men who die for Rome must get their land. It says: An end is coming.

CURIO: Of what?

CAESAR: That it does not say. I ask: Of me? Of the Republic? Of the law? No answer. Whoever has the answer must be God. And I must find an answer.

CURIO: Oh, Caesar. The answer's here. Not there in Rome. No one can give answer any more but Caesar, who holds the legions.

CAESAR: (*Drawing away from the group, rising to level of parapet, putting a height above them*) You mean . . . Caesar . . . to act for God? Only Asians confuse the men with Gods.

HIRTIUS: (*Dolefully shaking his head, as if it were a serious question*) It goes against the rules. But Curio's right. No one has the answer. Pompey has no answer. Nor Cato. Nor Cicero. Nor the families.

Nor the Senate. They cannot see a way to settlement.

CAESAR: Then, take it to the people then. . . . The people in Assembly . . . when they assemble in the Forum and cast their vote, they speak for the Gods.

BALBUS: Of course, of course . . . the people speak for the Gods. Only sometimes they are confused, do not understand what the Gods want of them.

CURIO: Caesar . . . you have been in Gaul nine years. These people are not the Roman people as you knew them.

HIRTIUS: He is right, Caesar. I did not believe last month; but you sent me on this mission; and this visit two weeks ago. All was changed, so changed I could not believe I was in Rome. Ten years ago, a voting mob was a crowd of drifting loafers, bored, looking for a day of games, or riot, a way to make a penny.

CURIO: It's different now. They're organized, these mobs. Cato pays for one, Pompey for another, we pay for ours. These are legions of the street, more dangerous than Gauls or Germans—

BALBUS: What was the people, Caesar, now is mobs.

CURIO: (*Resuming narrative, as Hirtius and Balbus from time to time interrupt, explaining. As they do, Caesar leaves the elevation of the parapet and steps down to join them in conference.*) It changed so fast. You left for Gaul, the Senate angry. You taught the people to think they could make law.

HIRTIUS: Clodius taught them that. I knew we couldn't trust Clodius. . . .

CURIO: Clodius tore it loose. He was your tribune of the people, in charge of collegia, workingmen's association, tribal captains, voting blocs.

BALBUS: He was not loyal, Caesar, not loyal.

CURIO: I was against Clodius—against you, too, Caesar, you remember.

CAESAR: I know. It cost me dear to buy you over as my tribune. . . .

CURIO: To buy the votes to *make* me tribune. Then I began to understand what happened to your Clodius. Tribune stands before the people in Assembly, voicing their demands against the Senate. You flatter them. They cheer. Their cheers blow up your thinking, tug it after them. You think you hold them in your hand. But they hold you, their cheers make you drunk. . . . Clodius loved the cheers, the shouting, the frenzy.

BALBUS: He thought *he* was Caesar. I begged him not to pass the law to exile Cicero. I told him Caesar did not want it done. But he had *his* score to settle with Cicero—

CURIO: Clodius packed the Forum for that vote—as they will do when you are tried, Caesar. The mob yelled, cheered, hooted—and Cicero was exiled. Cicero cried, he wept like a child. And they laughed.

BALBUS: Two years later, the same people cried and cheered to see him back. That was after the Senate had learned—they bought Milo to organize their gangs, as you bought Clodius.

CURIO: Milo hired gladiators, knifemen, clubmen. The Senate paid. And brought back Cicero. They killed at random, in street and alley. By night and day, in open riot and ambuscade by dark. Until Milo's knifemen caught Clodius on the road and killed him.

CAESAR: I did not want it that way . . . you know I did not want it that way.

BALBUS: I knew, I knew. . . . But then, when Clo-

dius died, his gangs boiled up. Caesar . . . no foreign enemies burned down the Senate House that
night two years ago. Romans put the torch to the
Senate. Even Clodius, alive, would not have dared to
burn the Senate. The Senators still mumble—it was
Caesar's mob.

CURIO: I am only three weeks quit with being tribune
of the people. Some mobs are bought—you pay for
them. And other mobs will crowd the Forum out of
hunger. The worst are mobs that come themselves,
like animals. For these you need the flat of sword—
or else its bloody tip. When I was young they used to
riot in Suburra, where the workers live. They used to
kill each other, and burn down houses.

CAESAR: (*Very calm, clinical*) Yes. They like a
flame. The fire's exciting.

CURIO: Now excitement calls them on. They pour
down from the gully of Suburra, down from the
hills, and burn inside the central city, in the Forum.
And you cannot stuff them back until you put the
flat of sword against their back. . . .

BALBUS: Or point of sword into their stomach.

CURIO: That is what the Senate's learned. To use the
sword against the mob. Only, since the Senate has no
sword, it must use Pompey's sword. Senate and Pompey hate each other. But they need each other. . . .

BALBUS: And Antony drives them closer, binds them
tight.

HIRTIUS: This is so. He angers Pompey.

CURIO: He is fresh in office.

HIRTIUS: And everyone was talking, when I left, of
his first Assembly. Stood before the people in Assembly and promised—all. Denounced Pompey. Spat on

Pompey's dignity. On Cicero. On Cato. On Senate.
And they cheered.

CURIO: He spoke to our mob, and thought it was the
people. They made him drunk with cheers. But on
voting day, Pompey's soldiers will be there with their
swords, and they will hush. Unless our sword is there
as well.

CAESAR: (*Sternly, now back in a tactical mood*) Antony *must* not do that. We still seek some arrangement with old Pompey.

CURIO: Antony does not care. Antony is action. Antony has a flag. Its name is Caesar. He does not know
how to seek accommodation. Once he plants the flag
in Pompey's body, then Caesar must redeem the flag.

CAESAR: (*Abruptly*) Pompey   must   trust   us.
(*Pauses.*) Or trust whoever speaks for me. Pollio!

POLLIO: Sir?

CAESAR: Go. Bring Labienus to me. He was not
altogether wrong. Tell him Caesar wants to speak to
him alone.

(*Exit Pollio.*)

CAESAR: (*Ruminating, to Curio*) You're sure? No
way of reaching voters except by leave of Pompey—
or the sword.

CURIO: No way. The people is a mob. It needs excitement. Or a sword.

CAESAR: Or some belief that makes it more than
mob.

CURIO: The people now believe in nothing. Only
more. More of everything. When Caesar ran for consul, he promised land. But Caesar now has conquered
Gaul, and Germany, and Britain. The city is swollen
with the wealth and spoils of conquest. It glitters all

about. They want the glitter; but not the land that must be worked.

CAESAR: My soldiers want their land.

CURIO: But they cannot come to vote.

CAESAR: I promised them their land and vote.

HIRTIUS: We cannot do it by the laws of Rome, unless they march to Rome to vote—against the rules.

CAESAR: Again, again.

(*In agony, seated*)

What am I to do? It is as if I were a river, a stream on which men choose to sail their boats. They choose the stream because they think it flows the way they want to go. They use me, all. My soldiers, tired of war, mercenaries most, think of themselves as patriots. But what they want is land. Labienus wants to stand with me for consulship. The way men used to stand for honor and for dignity, the seal of glory for something finished. Yet we are not finished, we must begin. Balbus, here—

(*Turns to Balbus.*)

What does Balbus want? He wants to be a senator, the first Spanish senator in Roman history. If Caesar triumphs, Balbus is a senator.

(*Balbus smiles—if he were a dog, he would wag his tail.*)

CAESAR: (*Points to Rome*) And Antony. Antony is with me because he likes the sense of action. A good soldier. But attacks too fast. If I should lose, Antony is nothing. If I should win—of course, a province of his own. Then—who knows what Antony dreams of? (*To Curio*)

And Curio, Curio—what does Curio want? Command and wealth? Consul in some future year? Estates? Curio, too, wants to float along the stream. No man cost me more than Curio to buy . . . but what I paid was money. Money never satisfies. Money is a first installment, what more must come?

CURIO: Caesar has paid me well. But money is not what binds me now. I have been too often back and forth across the Senate floor. With Pompey, with the Senate; against Caesar, for Caesar. And now I want a sense of peace.

CAESAR: And yet you counsel war.

CURIO: I wanted the Republic strong. And quiet in the city. I tried both ways. If the others win, they will remember only when I stood against them, and Caesar—

CAESAR: If Caesar wins—

CURIO: Caesar knows what to remember—and what to forget. I have no choice. No Gods will save me if Caesar is brought to trial and loses. I must believe in Caesar.

CAESAR: Pollio should write this down. Pollio? What does Pollio want? (*Peers at the group. Pollio is absent. Caesar recollects why Pollio is gone.*) Pollio! Where is Pollio? And Labienus? (*Yelling*) Pollio! (*Pause.*) All Pollio wants of Caesar is a story. A writer needs a neat symmetrical balance to his story. He needs some simple truth, a tree, with branches branching neatly, from which the twigs and leaves go forth in order. For Pollio, I must bring an order to his story. Order. For Rome as well—they need an order. Pollio!

(*Enter Pollio.*)

POLLIO: (*Perplexed*)   He's gone. He's left.

CAESAR: Who?

POLLIO: Labienus.

CAESAR: No. He cannot leave. I told him go and think. He's strolling. In the market. Or among the troops. Send messengers to fetch him.

POLLIO: I would. But can't. He left this message.

(*Caesar snatches the wax tablet from Pollio.*)

CAESAR: (*Reading*) "Titus Labienus to Gaius Julius Caesar. Salutes. Caesar has said: Go think. I go to think. I can no longer think in Caesar's presence. I must consult the Gods."

HIRTIUS: He's gone to Rome!

POLLIO: All else is there in chambers. His baggage, spoils, trophies. All remains behind. I asked. He rode off on his horse. Alone.

CURIO: Caesar! We must be after him. He is just five minutes gone. If he has gone to Rome, to ask the Gods their will—he'll not be back. Whatever works in Labienus' heart, in Rome they'll see him otherwise. Labienus is Caesar's chief-of-staff and runningmate for consul. If he abandons Caesar—

BALBUS: If Labienus leaves from Caesar's camp, it is desertion. In Rome, I know the way they read— they'll read that all of Caesar's army quits. Bring him back!

CAESAR: (*Calmly, reading the tablet again*) No. Hirtius—give orders. See that all his baggage follows him. Every silver plate. Swords and armor. Every trophy from the Rhine, Britain, Alesia. Pack it and speed it after him. It must arrive at the Rubicon before he does. With this message—Pollio, write it. (*Caesar moves and steps up to parapet platform, separating himself from the group. Pollio pulls out wax tablet. Caesar dictates as if from afar.*) "Caesar, Imperator. To Labienus, Legate. Salutes. Caesar

wishes Labienus well. Labienus has forgotten what
he won. Thus Caesar sends Labienus' trophies, all his
treasures, to the Rubicon, waiting his arrival. Caesar's
soldiers cannot cross the Rubicon. Else Caesar would
have sent what Labienus earned to Rome."

CURIO: No. Caesar, no! Labienus destroys all chance
of bargain. Not Senate, not Pompey, not Assembly,
no one will listen if they think that Caesar's own army
turns against him. Bring him back.

CAESAR: (*Not hearing anyone*) The message to go
instantly with this baggage. See to it. It is six hours
here to the Rubicon and Labienus will not hurry, for
he is troubled. . . .

CURIO: It will not bring him back, once they talk
to him in Rome—once he learns they can make him
consul without Caesar—

CAESAR: (*Very remote on the parapet; stage lights
slowly dim.*) I do not want him back. Who follows
Caesar must believe in Caesar. Labienus was too close
to me; he saw Caesar too close for real belief. He
could not dream.

(*Spotlight on Caesar—very gaunt, melancholy, bitter, but certain of himself, and proud*)

Yet he grew from my dreams, as the nails of my fingers grow from my body. I cut him from me, now,
as when I peel dead horn. I shall miss the cutting edge
he gave command. But no pain.

(*Pause.*)

Yes, a little pain for memory. For what has gone before. When we were friends and partners. More pain
for what may come tomorrow. Labienus left to save
the law of Rome. If he succeeds—he is a hero and I
am safe. If not—then I must go on trial—and lose all

dignity, or die. Or act as God—in which case, the Republic dies. And Labienus, who sought as I to save it, also dies. For his death—I have sorrow, pain. He was too close. No one must be close.

(*Caesar stands dim-lit on parapet, his voice distant but ringingly clear.*)

No more of counsel.

(*Pauses, looks around.*)

Caesar speaks. Orders. Hirtius—pass command. Nightly now, at first dark, then again at midnight— test the signal fires. Alert across the Alps—by Como, Galba's Pass. Grenoble. Viennorum to the Rhone and Fabius. Alert! No man moves until I say. But alert. Go now. Pass command.

(*Exit all, leaving Caesar alone. Caesar turns south, to Rome, and, in a voice rising from plea to denunciation, finally shouting, speaks from parapet to the darkness.*)

Listen! Listen, I tell you. Rome, listen! Let me come and speak to you. Do you hear me? I am a citizen of Rome. I do not want to be a God. *Do not want to be a God.* I want to talk to you. There must be change, I tell you. I know. There must be order as we change. Let me explain. Let me come to you. Not as Sulla. Not as victim. Not as God. Let me talk. Without a sword. Do not make me be a God. Do not make me . . . listen . . . listen . . . do you hear me?

(*As he ends in a shriek, the first signal fire flares.*)

Do you see? Romans, do you see?

(*Signal flares again.*)

Listen! Listen!

(*His voice is drowned in cheers, boos, catcalls, shriekings, mob sounds from out the darkness.*)

Those are legions' fires! Your legions. Our legions.
My legions. I do not want to use them. Caesar does
not want to be a God!

CURTAIN

ACT THREE

SCENE ONE

Time: December 27.
Place: The same.

Night scene: Beyond the balcony, moon and stars. Clouds scudding by; occasionally obscuring moon. Against the moonlight, Caesar on the balcony, silhouetted rigid and erect, peering at the sky. Caesar's back is to the audience as it is to Pollio—who now wanders in from far right.

POLLIO: (*As narrator*) And now, with Labienus gone, the week dissolved by days, the days vanished into hours, the hours slipped away by minutes. All of us tugged forward in our thoughts by the opening of the Senate session on the first.

What meaning would they read in Labienus' flight? What program would the consuls put before the house? And we had none.

Except to stick with law until the law struck us. Resting our hopes on restless Antony in Rome—our only fingergrip on law; he, as tribune of Assembly and of people, fresh in office, still entitled to veto any Senate act until proposed and passed by people in the Forum.

What to tell him? What to say?

C A E S A R :   (*Turning, slowly, but not leaving his place on the balcony*)   Is Curio ready?

P O L L I O :   Yes, sir. They're packing his bags. He'll be here in a minute.

C A E S A R :   Good. (*Turns back to stare at stars, as clouds pass.*) You know, they're out of place.

P O L L I O :   What, sir?

C A E S A R :   The stars. Come here. (*Pollio joins Caesar on balcony. Caesar points.*) Castor there. Scorpio there. Those stars say it's November.

P O L L I O :   But sir—the Saturnalia's over. It's the end of December.

C A E S A R :   So the calendar says—but the stars *still* say November.

P O L L I O :   Is that bad, sir?

C A E S A R :   Good—and bad. Good for us, now. Early November, say the stars—so the passes in the Alps are not yet full of snow. Once the Alpine passes block with snow, we have no way of bringing Fabius' legions here till spring. Too late.

P O L L I O :   I saw snow this morning, sir.

C A E S A R :   A November flurry. Pray it waits. The days still grow shorter, the nights longer. It's not December yet, no matter what the calendar says. It's off the pace. And that's bad.

P O L L I O :   The *calendar*, sir? Off pace?

C A E S A R :   The calendar. Fifty-odd days off its pace since I've been away. Nine years away. The High Priest sets the calendar, you know. It shouldn't need a High Priest to set the months in seasons by the mysteries.

P O L L I O :   But the seasons slip around so much, sir—

someone has to fix their place.

CAESAR: They should be fixed in order. So should the calendar. Once—forever.

POLLIO: (*Not comprehending*) *Forever?* The same calendar *every* year?

CAESAR: In Egypt, there is a Greek called Sosigenes. A scholar who watches stars. He says the sun goes around the earth each year, one circle every three hundred and sixty-five days. To be exact: three hundred sixty-five days, six hours, some minutes more or less. When we find him, we will fix the calendar forever.

POLLIO: Yes, sir—I'm for it.

CAESAR: Fix it all. One new calendar for all the world of Rome. The year must *not* begin in March, when planting begins along the Tiber. Planting begins at different times in Britain, Gaul, Italy, Sicily, Africa, Egypt. March is a very bad month to start a year.

POLLIO: When *should* it begin, sir?

CAESAR: In winter. At the solstice, when the day begins to grow again. *That's* the same everywhere. First new moon after the sun starts back. The calendar must be the same for all the world—and the language, and the law, and the beginning of the year . . .

POLLIO: That would be the first of January. Seems odd, doesn't it, to have a New Year begin in January. That's next week. . . .

CAESAR: Three days from now. We will not fix the calendar this week, Pollio, there are more important things to do this year. (*Strides out from balcony. Impatiently*) Now, where is Curio, he should be off. (*Bawls out*) Curio! Curio! (*Paces as he waits, and*

Pollio follows him, busy scribbling with stylus.) All
of it, all of it, the world has grown too big for village sorcery—or else too small. All of it must be fixed.
The sky has order, the stars have order—so must
men.

(*Enter Curio with Hirtius.*)

Ah, Curio—sit. Hirtius—sit. You are ready?

CURIO: Ready, Caesar. The horse is saddled.

CAESAR: (*Peremptorily*) Fresh horses all the way—
no sleep until you get to Rome, Curio. You must be
there before the Senate opens on the first. Sleep when
you have gotten there. Sleep at Antony's. He is
guarded.

HIRTIUS: He'll be difficult. He won't like the message.

CAESAR: I know he won't.

CURIO: But who speaks for Caesar? Antony or I?

CAESAR: You speak first. For peace. You understand
the mission?

CURIO: The Senate meets at noon. I sit as close as possible to Antony behind the tribune's bench.

CAESAR: Lentulus, as senior consul, opens the session.
He will bring in some resolution on the state. He is
wax in the hands of the faction. The resolution will
be against us. Antony, in the name of the Assembly
and the people, will intervene against a roll-call, insisting the Senate first hear Caesar's proposal. You
have the letter?

CURIO: I have it here. (*Pulls out of toga a packet of
papyrus.*)

CAESAR: Antony wins you right of hearing on the
floor—and then you read my letter. Mark you—*you*
read it; gently; sweetly; the words are clear. If

Antony reads it, it will sound like threat. *You* read
it.

HIRTIUS: Ever so gently . . . with ever so many
"conscript fathers" . . . ever so many appeals to
their wisdom . . . ever so many "honored this" and
"reverend that."

CAESAR: They must be soothed. Drawn back to
think again. A month ago, they voted that Pompey
and I both must yield command. Make clear how
readily I now accept their judgment. I yield. All my
troops, all my legions, both commands, Gaul-Beyond-
the-Alps and Gaul-Within-the-Alps. I accept the
authority of the Senate.

CURIO: (*Disturbed, uneasy*) We should sound
stronger.

CAESAR: Read it soft. As if I beg of them: that all
accept the same authority. And ask: Will they insist
that Pompey, too, lay down his arms? Will they consult their conscience, defy both Cato and the *nobiles*,
and let me go before the people without harm?

HIRTIUS: This is the delicate part.

CAESAR: *Most* delicate: You must rouse the Senate
sheep against their leaders. With leaders present and,
perhaps, Pompey's troops outside. Caesar bows to
their will, not to Cato or the *nobiles*—agrees to protect them, or lay down arms, their will be done. We
stick on law alone. The law gives me command until
March first. In those eight weeks within the shelter of
the law, I hold—and seek arrangement.

CURIO: I have it here, I'll do my best.

CAESAR: Any role they wish, I'll play. Except but
one—I will not be a victim. I'll chance the mobs, the
gangs, the Forum, vote matching vote in Fifth Month

elections. But they must not try Rome's Highest
Priest—the Gods forbid, and I forbid.

CURIO: And if they refuse?

CAESAR: Then Antony will speak. But you speak
first. Erase their fears. The danger that they fear is in
my mind alone. If I move first, their danger's real, the
law with them. I will not move.

CURIO: And if they move first?

CAESAR: Ah—if *they* move first? They would not be
such fools. . . .

HIRTIUS: I'm not so sure. With Labienus preceding
Curio to Rome, gossip spreading overnight—Caesar's
generals desert, his army mutinies—

CAESAR: Sad Labienus—who hopes for peace. If he
lets them make such reading of his act, then he will
trouble peace far more than he has troubled me.

CURIO: How so, Caesar?

CAESAR: If his return persuades them that I mean to
march, yet cannot because my generals revolt; if they
beguile themselves to strike, *before* I move, then *they*
have breached the law—and force is free for use by
every man. You have not seen a battle yet, my Curio
—nor should you wish to see one. Go for peace.
Then—if you fail—

CURIO: Then what?

CAESAR: You have the choice of Labienus, still—to
be with Caesar or the law. Be careful now of Antony
—he wants to strike, you must restrain him.

CURIO: I feel myself at heart, this once, with Antony.

CAESAR: (*Wearily*) It would make a fine tale, would
it not, if I struck. But let me say it one last time before
we cast the dice: To strike, one needs an object. I do

not want for spoils, honor, gold. My object is to do
what must be done—for this I need the cloak of law,
the garment of legitimacy. To seize the city's not
enough. I need what's *in* the city—whatever magic's
left to law. I need the Senate *there*, when I am consul.
Hostile, sullen, cowed, bribed, seduced, however they
will—I need consent. If I strike, I scatter them, scatter
what I seek. Perhaps a pounce, a swoop might do it.
But that's last chance of all the chances I must dare.

CURIO: But what if we *must* pounce—when would I
know? What must I do?

CAESAR: That depends on what you find in Rome.
You will keep me informed. There will be four messengers a day—right?

HIRTIUS: Yes, Caesar, all arranged.

CAESAR: All messages—in code.

HIRTIUS: Done, Caesar—the codes are ready.

CAESAR: And the signal fires. You understand them,
Curio?

CURIO: Not quite.

CAESAR: (*Mounts to third tier.*)   Come here—all of
you. (*They gather about him.*) Pollio—raise a fire
from the platform. (*Pollio leaves. Caesar points directly out from balcony—south.*) One hundred eighty
miles—here to Rome. (*Caesar leans over, pointing to
stage left, to Gaul.*) Four hundred twenty miles,
across the Alps, to Fabius. (*To Curio*) These fires are
what we learned from fighting Gauls. Two years ago
when they last rose—they flared such signals from the
hills, hill to hill, from Orleans north to Soissons, west
to Aquitaine, south to Lyons. One night they flared
—next dawn, from end to end of Gaul, they rose and

slaughtered Roman settlers, garrisons. Labienus cut off in the north, and I away . . .

CURIO: Labienus understands these signals, too?

CAESAR: (*Mournfully*) He knows. We learned to-gether. But different lessons. . . . From every enemy defeated one must learn—Ah, there. . . . (*Flare goes up in wings of stage.*) We have improved on what the Gauls taught us . . . but still so crude . . . yet so much quicker than messengers. For example, to Fabius on the Rhone—one long blaze, one short blaze, one long blaze, three times over—means march! Three short blazes, thrice repeated—means alert, but stay still.

CURIO: And for us? How do I speak to you from Rome?

CAESAR: For us? More difficult. Because messages in fire are coarse, and the problem in Rome, subtle. Balbus has fire-codes in Rome. Simple codes for names, places, numbers; codes for "wait, messengers on the way," "hope," "no hope." Longer codes for words and letters—but fires arouse attention, the longer codes are dangerous . . . and Labienus' there— Ah, you see . . . (*Caesar leans over balcony, as the flares begin to rise and fall in sequence. A great orange light begins to wink at far right of balcony, offstage. Its three short bursts, followed by three more, followed by three more, continue as Caesar goes on with conversation.*) Three short blazes. The alert—all's well, but alert. It will take three hours for the signals to reach Fabius. Half that time for your signals to get to me from Rome.

CURIO: I pray I send all's well.

CAESAR: (*As the last burst of flame dies out offstage*)

Pray all the Gods. . . . So crude a way to talk, these
fire signals. Someday men will talk across the mountains, rivers, oceans, instantly. If I could only *talk* to
Rome. Or use a star to signal with.

CURTAIN

SCENE TWO

TIME: Ten days later, January 7, 49 B.C.
PLACE: The same.

(*Enter Pollio.*)

POLLIO: (*As narrator*) So we waited those last ten days. With all the legions of the north ready at the signal of our flares, we waited—powerless.

Watching the southern hills for flares. Waiting each day the panting messengers; but always knowing the news they brought was two days old, already history: Senate had met on January first. Heard Caesar's message. Argued. Screamed. Raged across the floor. Pompey's troops brought up to ring the Senate. Then Pompey wavered, hesitated, might want to talk. So the Senate wavered, hesitated, might want to talk. Then Cato thundered—and Pompey firmed, so the Senate firmed. Against us.

On January fourth, the first hard news. A resolution carried on Scipio's motion—that Gaius Julius Caesar must give up all command, *imperium*, the scarlet cloak, on the fixed day.

The fixed day—*certam diem*. But what fixed day?

When? Before our legal term expired or not? They argued. And then Mark Antony was talking, not Curio. Some wavered—urged a conference. Cato thundered that the Senate of Rome negotiates with no individual—another motion, on the morning of the fifth, carried: Domitius Ahenobarbus to replace Caesar in Gaul; Syria for the Scipios; Mauretania for Faustus Sulla—the looting begun before the peace was made.

Our latest courier with news: Antony insisting such new appointments to command must be ratified by vote of people, in Assembly, in the Forum. A lawyer's point—but legal. A play for time. Else Antony will veto.

We waited in Ravenna, just the three of us, Caesar, Hirtius and myself. Antony, Curio, Balbus in Rome. Labienus gone. The legions in Gaul—all packed, at ready. And he—never so gay or easy.

(*Curtain opens. Caesar sprawled in ease beside the mensa, on a lounging couch. Occasionally he eats a grape or two; occasionally he rattles his dice in a silver dice cup and idly casts them; this rattling of dice is his only show of nerves.*)

(*Hirtius is pacing back and forth, front-stage, in obvious agitation: pulling on his nose, scratching his head, all a-twitch, violently. Pollio is reading from a scroll which he winds and re-winds constantly. It is the great best-seller of the day—Cicero's* De Re Publica—*a proposal for constitutional reform.*)

CAESAR: . . . and Cicero expects grown-up people to listen to *this?*

POLLIO: Everyone is reading it. Atticus' slave-scribes publish, they say, no less than twenty copies of *De Re*

Publica a week—and all are sold.

CAESAR: To students, perhaps; or teachers. But men who must govern have no time to read of government. . . . Well, anyway, *we* have time today, go on with the reading.

POLLIO: (*Reading*) "A commonwealth is the property of a people. But a people is not any collection of human beings brought together in any sort of way, but an assemblage of people associated in an agreement with respect to justice and partnership for common good. . . ."

CAESAR: That Cicero will outlive us all. History belongs to writers. The large mind, the jeweled phrase. Always the clarifying definitions that light up all . . . it is only the stroke of action Cicero cannot grasp.

HIRTIUS: (*Stopping his pacing*) Cicero's *there*, he's there in *Rome* now.

CAESAR: Yes, I know. But he has no troops—nor votes.

HIRTIUS: We should have tried to reach him.

CAESAR: We did. But when the issue comes to vote —he will offer philosophy, and vote with the majority. He cried, remember, when they voted him into exile—cried and sobbed in public, but obeyed because it was a law. Came back a broken man. And tries now to win by letters what he lost by vote.

HIRTIUS: Today's the seventh. They vote again today, what are they saying—(*In agitation, in his pacing, stumbles over a footstool, sprawls, pulls himself up.*)

CAESAR: Hirtius, stop twitching! You look nervous!

HIRTIUS: I *am* nervous!

CAESAR: If it pleases you—*be* nervous. But don't make me nervous. Go on, Pollio.

POLLIO: Where was I? (*Rolls up the scroll, unwinds again to find his place. He is nervous too.*)

CAESAR: Get to some answers. This is supposed to be the solution to constitutional crisis—so far it is only definitions. Everyone is brilliant making definitions.

POLLIO: Well, then he goes on . . . (*Rattling the scroll*) "Thus, between the weakness of a single ruler, and the rashness of the mass, aristocracies have occupied that intermediate position which represents the utmost moderation. In a state ruled by its best men, the citizens must necessarily enjoy the greatest happiness, being freed from all cares and worries—"

CAESAR: (*Interrupting*) That will please the Senate, all right. But he doesn't say how you find the best men, does he? Find answers!

HIRTIUS: (*Interjecting*) Answers! We need answers right now! Caesar, we must *do* something.

CAESAR: (*Casting his dice*) We are.

HIRTIUS: What?

CAESAR: The hardest thing—waiting. (*Casts dice— peers, picks up dice, yawns.*) Sooner or later, one of us must make a mistake. They in Rome—or I, here.

HIRTIUS: But what if Domitius Ahenobarbus arrives, now, in Ravenna—and tells the troops that the Senate has given him command, that you are summoned in civil toga to Rome?

CAESAR: (*Grandiloquently*) We will treat him as our guest. We will point out how rude and unjust it would be for Domitius to address this legion without permission of its legal commander. We would have to do our duty—as he his. What is that, Pollio, you just read in Cicero—about duty?

P O L L I O :　(*Dutifully reading*) "For we must choose one of three things—to do injustice and not to suffer it; or both to do it and to suffer it; or else neither to do it, nor to suffer it!"

C A E S A R :　(*Airily*) Not that, he wanders too much—about the different laws.

P O L L I O :　"If it is the duty of a just and good man to obey the laws, what laws is he to obey? All the different laws that exist?"

C A E S A R :　Just so. We would discuss Domitius' duty and mine. His law and mine. But Domitius will not come.

H I R T I U S :　He will. Someone will come.

C A E S A R :　No. They want to take me. But to take the lion as he growls needs more than words—it takes strength. To make such strength takes time. If we wait, they will blunder. Hirtius, dear friend, I love you—but if you do not enjoy the readings, you may go.

(*Hirtius drags out, nervous and fretful.*)

C A E S A R :　Go on, Pollio, read on.

P O L L I O :　He quotes from Plato here, it's better, about liberty.

C A E S A R :　Let's hear the Greek.

P O L L I O :　(*Resuming*) "When liberty prevails everywhere, it follows that the vice of anarchy extends even to domestic animals, until finally father fears son, son flouts his father, the schoolmaster flatters and fears his pupils, pupils despise their masters, all is so absolutely free that wives have the same rights as their husbands, and in the abundance of liberty, even the dogs, the horses and the asses are so free in their running about that men must make way for them in the streets."

CAESAR: We'll have to fix the traffic in Rome, of course.

POLLIO: (*Continuing*) "The final result of this boundless license is that the minds of the citizens become so squeamish and sensitive that, if the authority of government is exercised in the slightest degree, they become angry and cannot bear it. . . ." (*As Pollio reads, his voice trails off and finally he breaks.*) Oh, Caesar, I am nervous, too.

CAESAR: Ah, young Pollio, you must learn: You may let yourself be nervous. But never say it. Or show it. Fear has a smell. (*Casts dice, lets them roll on floor, stoops, examining them.*) See, twin-eyes . . . it came up Venus! I always win when I play alone. (*Rises.*) Put Cicero away. No one can teach government from a book.

POLLIO: No?

CAESAR: Books on politics teach probabilities. But government is art.

POLLIO: Art?

CAESAR: An art in use of men. No book can teach it. You were not there at the siege of Bourges. The Gauls had tallow-throwers on the walls. They stepped up, one after the other, their pots of tallow flaming as they flung it on our siege machinery. Each time a Gaul was outlined on the wall—one single moment for our archers to sight and shaft him. One after the other—they stood, threw, were shafted, fell dying from the wall. Four times, by Hercules, four men. One man after the other—stood, threw, was killed, tumbled.

POLLIO: (*By now he has his tablet out, taking notes*) Yes?

CAESAR: Brave men. Free men. We destroyed them —while all the other Gauls, in camp across the range, stood by waiting to fight only when *their* chieftains gave the word. Each tribe, each family, a law to itself. Tribesmen—not a nation. This is the art, Pollio—to make men strive like free, yet bind them in an order that gives the freedom strength.

POLLIO: Like Rome . . .

CAESAR: Like Rome was long ago—bound by a faith, a trust, a magic glue that makes, as Cicero says, a commonwealth. And now, in Rome, the glue is old. Brittle. At the slightest shake, it cracks. So we must find another glue—if not me, another.

(*Enter Hirtius, rushing, agitated.*)

HIRTIUS: Caesar! Caesar! Signal flares!

CAESAR: (*Coolly*) From west or south?

HIRTIUS: From south—Rome!

CAESAR: (*Rises abruptly, commanding*) Acknowledge.

(*Red flare on balcony is already beginning to glow.*)

HIRTIUS: I have. That's our acknowledgment now.

(*Pollio has rushed to the balcony, peering south. Hirtius follows. Caesar remains down-stage center.*)

CAESAR: It reads?

POLLIO: (*From balcony. He is deciphering slowly. He reads to Hirtius, who repeats very loudly, casting his voice to Caesar.*) "Antony . . ."

HIRTIUS: (*Repeating*) Antony . . .

POLLIO: ". . . and Curio . . ."

HIRTIUS: . . . and Curio . . .

POLLIO: ". . . and Cassius . . ."

HIRTIUS: . . . and Cassius . . .

POLLIO: ". . . have fled . . ."

HIRTIUS: . . . have fled . . .

POLLIO: I don't know, can't read it, maybe just they've left.

HIRTIUS: Or left.

CAESAR: (*Curtly*) Get on with it!

POLLIO: ". . . have fled the city . . ."

HIRTIUS: . . . have fled the city . . .

POLLIO: ". . . for Ravenna . . ."

HIRTIUS: . . . for Ravenna—they're coming back!

POLLIO: ". . . The Senate . . ."

HIRTIUS: . . . The Senate . . .

POLLIO: ". . . today . . ."

HIRTIUS: . . . today . . .

POLLIO: (*After a long minute of waiting*) There's a break there in the signal.

HIRTIUS: (*Turning now to join him, peering south*) There *is* a break . . . no further signals.

CAESAR: Query them. Give them a flash.

(*The fire on balcony is already doing so.*)

HIRTIUS: We are. Our signals are querying. . . . There. There's something. . . .

POLLIO: (*Reading the flares*) "Message . . ."

HIRTIUS: Message . . .

POLLIO: ". . . cut off . . ."

HIRTIUS: . . . cut off . . .

POLLIO: ". . . at signal end in Rome."

HIRTIUS: . . . at signal end in Rome. They've broken the message. They were caught.

C A E S A R :   I suppose so. I'm surprised Labienus didn't cut us off sooner. (*Strides to balcony, and shouts up to signal station on roof.*) Ho, up there! Ho, signalers!

(*Answering shout from on top; and thereafter, the messages flare quite rapidly.*)

C A E S A R :   Send this . . .

H I R T I U S :   (*Almost trembling*) To Gaul, Caesar— to Fabius?

C A E S A R :   (*Turning to Hirtius*) No, this one goes south. (*Turns back and shouts as if his voice reaches all the way to Rome.*) A message south . . . for Titus Labienus. . . . (*Signals go.*) "Old friend" . . . (*Shouting*) . . . "fare well." . . . (*Shouting*) Do you have that? That's all. . . . Give the Gallic signature: "From Gaius Julius Caesar. Imperator." (*Caesar returns center stage. He is still composed, but now his head is held very high, and rigid.*)

P O L L I O :   And now—to Gaul? We march?

C A E S A R :   We sit. To Gaul no change of signal. Alert. No more.

H I R T I U S :   That's all?

C A E S A R :   No more tonight. There's little longer now to wait. We walk along the knife's edge. Let's not slip. Two days more and we know what answer's left to us.

H I R T I U S :   We know now. Our men have fled. Oh, Caesar—do not let them gather first. We have only one legion here—that's all.

C A E S A R :   Our men have fled . . . or left . . . Nor do we know what final resolution the Senate took today. Two days more and Curio, Antony, Cassius will be here. I think they'll hurry.

HIRTIUS: So will the others racing after them. And after that, Pompey's troops . . .

CAESAR: So I hope. Today, someone has blundered. Either they . . . or I. (*Caesar takes out his dice and is idly casting, as curtain closes.*)

CURTAIN

SCENE THREE

TIME: The evening of January 10, 49 B.C.
PLACE: The same.

(*Enter Pollio.*)

POLLIO: (*As narrator*) I learned as much those last
three days as all the years before—when something
happens in our world of men, some one man, by will,
must make it happen. Spies all about us. They prying
for our secrets, to know our mind—just as our spies,
in Rome, pried theirs. Everyone watching him—the
townspeople, the troops, the officers. And he as smooth
and sunny as the surface of Lake Como in a calm.
Antony, Curio, Cassius had fled the seventh, at night.
We waited all the eighth and ninth. No news, no signals.
And the tenth. All day again. We did not dare to
speak to him. He called a banquet for the evening.
We gaped. He said that we were all too tense—
needed a party. Local wrestlers. Local dancers. Local
music—the best a small provincial town can summon.
And I to represent the poets.
Hirtius would not come. Too nervous to sit still.

Paced the balcony—as if his eyes could scratch from darkness one last signal lost in Rome, one last shred of hope. . . .

(*In background, sound of Roman music. Curtain opens. Hirtius alone, pacing; two guards below front stage.*)

HIRTIUS: Soldier!

FIRST SOLDIER: Sir?

HIRTIUS: Do you see anything down there?

FIRST SOLDIER: (*Approaching balcony*) It's too dark, sir. I can't see a thing. Where?

HIRTIUS: Coming up the hill. (*Turns to second soldier.*) You come here. (*Waits.*) Do you see anything?

SECOND SOLDIER: No, sir—too dark.

FIRST SOLDIER: I see something now, sir. A wagon —a farmer's wagon.

SECOND SOLDIER: Me, too.

HIRTIUS: No wagon should be on that road. There's curfew all the way from here to Rubicon—sentries on patrol.

FIRST SOLDIER: That's right.

SECOND SOLDIER: (*Still peering*) Coming to the gate. Someone getting out. (*Pause.*) He fell. (*Pause.*) He's trying to run. He's tired. He's limping.

HIRTIUS: (*To first soldier*) Tell Caesar—a messenger. (*As he goes, Hirtius recalls him.*) No. He'll think I'm nervous. Call Pollio. (*To second soldier*) Get down there. Pass him instantly through the gates. Bring him here. Go. (*Soldier leaves. Hirtius returns to balcony, nervous as can be.*) They let him in. It *has* to be a messenger.

(*Enter Pollio.*)

POLLIO: A messenger, you said?

HIRTIUS: I don't know. Someone in a wagon.

POLLIO: Messengers don't come by wagon.

HIRTIUS: I don't care how they come. We need a messenger. How's Caesar?

POLLIO: Enjoying everything. Applauds the dancers as if they danced in Athens, the wrestlers as if they were the last turn in the theater—

HIRTIUS: He can enjoy anything, anytime.

POLLIO: Now he has a discourse going on poetry with the local learned men.

HIRTIUS: Poets upset him. He used to write himself when he was young. Says now that when he's consul he'll have every copy left in Rome burned— There! They're coming!

(*Enter Curio, limping on arm of Commander of the Guard, followed by soldier. Curio is, at first, almost unrecognizable. He is dressed in a brown tunic that looks like a long, dirty nightshirt, the garment of a slave. He is unshaven. Every move, as he drags himself to a chair, is one of exhaustion.*)

HIRTIUS: (*Who has been taken aback, now rushing to Curio, taking his arm from the centurion*) Curio! Curio! Oh, Curio, what news?

CURIO: (*Panting*) I . . . I . . . There is so much to tell. . . . Caesar?

HIRTIUS: (*Snapping orders to the Commander of the Guard, while Pollio pours a flask of wine for Curio, who sips, panting*) Commander! Tell Caesar Curio is here. Himself. (*Commander darts out.*) You others! (*To the soldiers*) Leave us! (*To Curio*) What happened? Oh, what's happened? Speak, man, speak.

CURIO: (*Haltingly*) They chased us. . . . Sentries on the roads . . . We had to come by the hills. . . .

We dressed as slaves. . . . No change of horses . . .
I fell. . . .

POLLIO: Where's Antony?

CURIO: At Rimini . . . with Cassius . . . just across
the Rubicon . . . garrison is friendly there. . . .

(*Enter Caesar in a splendid white robe. Enters briskly.
Pauses, startled at sight of Curio. Curio tries to rise,
stumbles. Caesar presses him down in chair.*)

CAESAR: You're hurt!

CURIO: Nothing, a bruise. Caesar . . . this is the
way it was in Rome.

CAESAR: How? Give me the heart of it!

CURIO: Outlaws. All of us. They outlawed us. (*Re-
laxing, talking slower, sipping wine as he talks, Curio
goes on with narration.*) We insisted, as you know,
until your legal term expired, no change of command
could come by Senate law—unless ratified by Assembly of the People. As you instructed.

CAESAR: Yes.

CURIO: Then, yesterday, no, not yesterday, no, the
day we left, the seventh—

HIRTIUS: The night they cut the signals.

CURIO: Labienus knew. He knew the codes, the fires.

CAESAR: (*Sharply*) I knew he knew. Go on.

CURIO: They began the mobilization. Divided Italy
all in districts—for recruiting of an army to defend
the state. We protested. Senate met in the Temple of
Jupiter. Antony, magnificent. We had three voices—
mine, Antony, Cassius. A hundred waverers. The
Senate raging. Cicero refusing to attend the meeting
—pleading from beyond the gate.

CAESAR: That men be wise and good and moderate,
I know. Get on with it.

CURIO: Pompey's troops around the Senate. Pompey not there—waiting to be called to duty—but Cato, Scipio, Domitius, all of them, talking as if Pompey's army was now theirs.

CAESAR: Garrison troops. Not an army, the fools.

CURIO: We vetoed mobilization. Antony exercising tribune's right of veto, Cassius joining him. They yelled. Were knives permitted on the Senate floor, they would have knifed us then. Fists balled. Curses. We held to law—

CAESAR: Good.

CURIO: Then. Up rose Gaius Marcellus. They had it planned—with every legal niceness. And proposed: SENATUS CONSULTUM ULTIMUM.

CAESAR: Consultum Ultimum? The final judgment? . . . The fools!

POLLIO: Consultum Ultimum—but isn't that for instant emergency?

CURIO: Last used two years ago . . . when the mobs burned the Senate down.

CAESAR: No—for any national emergency. Pollio's too young to remember. Used by the Senate when Cicero suppressed the Catiline conspiracy—fifteen years ago. Before that, unused in thirty years.

HIRTIUS: (*Agitated*) They had no right, I say, no right to use it . . . against the rules.

CAESAR: (*Calmly, explaining to Pollio, but really discovering what he thinks himself as he thinks aloud*) A very complicated legal point. The consul acts for Rome, with the advice of the Senate, to execute the laws passed by the people, who speak with the voice of the Gods. But if a national emergency impends; if an enemy is at the gates, in combat ranks; if the city is torn by riot so that laws cannot be passed. *If*—but only *if*—there is no time to act by law, and if survival of the State is at stake—then the consul may appeal to the Senate for Consultum Ultimum. And the Senate, in its wisdom, then gives its ultimate counsel, its supreme advice. It lifts the process of all law, puts direct decision, throughout the emergency, in the hands not only of the consul but of all legal magistrates, and those they call on to defend the state against its enemies.

CURIO: (*Resuming*) Antony rose next. Vetoed the proposal, and forbade a vote. The lawyers argued—could a veto legally intervene on Consultum Ultimum? Such noise and screaming. And all about, the city silent. Crowds in the Forum, silent. Soldiers at the entrance, silent. Only the Senate screaming. Could a tribune of the people forbid the proclamation of emergency? And then the threats: "Get off the floor"; "Get out." The roll-call readied. And if the roll-call passed—and now we knew it would. Then what? They could not seize us before the calling of the roll. But after that—the consul might arrest us as the agents of the enemy. Cato's face, livid, greedy for the act. Scipio, ready to pounce. We did not stay. But we did not run. Walked—slowly, oh so slowly. They would not kill us in the Hall of Jupiter. Thus, down the hill—and then we ran, changed costume, sought out horses, left at once. A skirmish at the bridge, the warrant for our seizure already issued—and got away.

CAESAR: And where is Antony? Where Cassius?

CURIO: They rest at Rimini, across the Rubicon. Antony and Cassius are still tribunes of the people.

No warrant has yet reached Rimini. And Caesar is quite close. The garrison there hesitates, uncertain. Antony and Cassius wait your word.

CAESAR: So. (*Long pause*) So. (*To Pollio*) Mark you, young historian, you get this right. Has any man of Caesar moved?

POLLIO: No, Caesar.

CAESAR: Has any legion moved from Gaul?

POLLIO: No, Caesar.

CAESAR: So nothing threatens Rome from this border. And Gaul is quiet. All the northland still because I stilled it. No threat to Rome from any foreign enemy. And in Rome, Curio? (*Turning to Curio*) No tumult? No riot in the street? No defilement of the images, no blood?

CURIO: For fifteen years, the streets of Rome have never known such quiet. Men gather in crowds—and whisper. Whispers louder than a roar.

CAESAR: (*Musing*) The voice of the people—choked. And the voice of the people is the voice of the Gods. The tribunes of Assembly, whose veto comes from the people, thus from the Gods, are hounded out as criminal. Is this not a breach of law? Or worse—is this not sacrilege? No one permitted to speak for people—or for Gods. And no man makes a protest?

CURIO: No man dares. The city shivers in its fear. Pompey's troops patrol the streets and Forum.

CAESAR: I, too, have troops.

CURIO: It is as if a cloud, the darkest cloud that man has ever seen, has settled on the city. As if the pillars of belief were shattered . . .

CAESAR: (*Slowly ascending the third tier of stage, to parapet, the distance growing between them*) And yet they must believe . . . or else there is no commonwealth. Must believe in something . . . or believe in someone. (*Turns abruptly, in change of mood, commanding. Pointing forefinger to Curio*) Command! Antony and Cassius are to wait at Rimini!

CURIO: How long?

CAESAR: Until they hear from me. Which will be quick. For I, too, am officer-of-state, until the first of March, a legal magistrate sworn to uphold the laws of Rome. And the Senate, in its wisdom, has declared emergency, lifting law. Each magistrate must now defend the law as conscience tell him to. (*Caesar whirls on Pollio.*) Pollio! My robes! Bring them at once. Do not interrupt the banquet. Louder music. More dancers. Say I will return. (*To others as Pollio leaves*) We are free now, all of us free to choose our roles. To choose the laws we want, the chieftains whom we trust, to fight like Gauls or Greeks among ourselves. You, too, are free—Hirtius, Curio, Pollio. And Antony, Cassius, Balbus, Labienus . . .

HIRTIUS: No, Caesar, no . . . I am Caesar's man.

CURIO: If I am free of Caesar, they will kill me dead—

CAESAR: All of you are free to go or stay. Not me. Caesar is not free. I am slave to every man. Slave to the legions who expect their land, to Gauls I stilled because I promised peace. As Rome itself must be a slave to all her conquests—shrunk to a single city in a world that grew from Rome. Slave as Caesar is to order. And who are greatest slaves of all?

HIRTIUS: Who, Caesar?

CAESAR: The greatest slaves are Gods. Tugged and
bound by prayers, dreams and hopes. Prisoners to
promises they never made. Gods—servants of slaves
who pray for freedom, of gamblers who pray the
dice fall right, of barren women who pray for children, of prisoners who pray for mercy, of soldiers
entering combat who pray for life. Most slave to
those who are most weak, who need an order and a
mercy most.

(*Turning his back to audience, face uplifted, praying*)
O Jupiter. And Mars. And Saturn. Apollo. Druids in
the groves. Invisible one of the Jews. If you were
there, I would not have to act as God. If you made
order as you should—it would not fall to me.

(*Caesar shakes his fist in passion at the sky.*)
I do what you should do because you will not do it.
(*Silence. In the silence enters Pollio carrying a brilliant sheaf of togas—the consular white, the saffron
yellow, the scarlet of imperial command.*)

POLLIO: Sir?

CAESAR: (*Slowly, turning, looking at him*) You
brought them all?

POLLIO: You did not say which one you wanted,
Imperator—I brought them all.

CAESAR: (*Stepping down, reaching for the robes.
Slowly lets the white toga of candidacy fall to the
ground*) White robe of stainless candidate. There'll
be no more of this except as mockery.

(*Fingering the saffron toga, as if reluctant to let it
go.*)
I am no longer priest to those who will not answer
me.

(*Lets toga slip to ground, steps on it, as he takes scarlet cape from Pollio.*)

Nor yet a God.

(*Hangs the scarlet cape over his arm, letting it float
out.*)

This helps men see. Blood always helps men see. So
does mercy. But first the blood—and then the mercy.
(*Turns to others, as he tucks the scarlet over his arm.
Carries it back with him, up to third tier.*)
The voice of the people has been choked. Two tribunes who speak for Gods and people have been hunted
out of Rome like criminals. Antony and Cassius sit
in Rimini denied their legal right of veto and the
Gods have been abused. I am magistrate, sworn to
protect the law. . . . Curio!

CURIO: Caesar!

CAESAR: (*He snaps all following commands.*)   The
messengers to Rimini, go now! To Antony and Cassius—to wait until tomorrow, Caesar marches to defend the law and rescue them. Go now! Hirtius!

HIRTIUS: Caesar!

CAESAR: Light the signals! To Gaul! Across the
Alps! To Fabius—say: March!

(*Exit Hirtius, running; Curio limps hastily after him.*)

CAESAR: Pollio!

POLLIO: Caesar!

CAESAR: Throw away your tablet. Find sword and
armor. Give orders in my name. Thirteenth Legion
assembles now at Ravenna to follow me; each cohort
marches to the Rubicon, in serial, the moment it is
stocked. But I must be across by dawn tomorrow
with the Praetorian cohort, Ensign of the Wolf.
Praetorian cohort mustered out of bed within the

hour. Instructions—speed. Fabius—speed. Trebonius
—speed. Speed you yourself to do my bidding. God-
speed.

(*Suddenly Caesar twirls the scarlet robe around him with
a brilliant flash of scarlet. Takes a pike from the pike-
stand and hurls it in fury against the wall—where it
quivers. And leaves stage in a blaze as signals now
begin to rise with a tremendous glow, flaring west
to Gaul. In this light,* Pollio *closes the play.*)

P O L L I O :   (*As narrator, stepping forward*) I loved
him. He did not want to be a God. Wanted to place
an order over things. But there was no place for him.
I wrote it. Everyone has used Pollio's history. I was
the only reporter with him when he crossed the
Rubicon. Exclusive story. Plutarch used my story,
so did Suetonius, Dio, Appian.
(*Pollio starts to leave the stage.*)
Oh, you want to know how it came out. Bloody, I
tell you. Pompey died. Then Cato—suicide in Africa,
wouldn't accept Caesar's mercy. Nor would Labienus
—killed in the last battle in Spain—fighting Caesar.
Those who surrendered—Caesar forgave, every one.
Then they assassinated him—and after that, they
called him God.
The others—well, later, Antony killed Hirtius. Also
Cicero. Curio got killed fighting in Africa. Later,
then, Caesar's nephew, Octavius, broke Antony, and
Antony killed himself in Egypt. Octavius called himself Augustus, claimed to be a God. He wasn't really,
only Caesar was a God. But Augustus knew how it
worked. It works this way—if men cannot agree on
how to rule themselves, someone else must rule them.

(*As curtain draws together, the last red flare calling the legions from Gaul dies down.*)

I have to hurry now. We cross the Rubicon at dawn. (*Exit Pollio.*)

CURTAIN

EPILOGUE

So CAESAR crossed the Rubicon; the Republic shivered at his touch; and fell. After which he soared completely out of the understanding of his time, ending as Dictator and God, master of the world.

It is one of the rare graceful gifts of history that the two most exciting voices which have come down to us from the days that followed should be those of the two greatest protagonists of the drama—Caesar and Cicero. Caesar's own story of the first two years of the Civil Wars carries the thrust of action and narrative. But Cicero's carries the attendant agony to its end. For Cicero was wedded to an idea—the idea of a Republic, and it was an idea that Caesar had killed, a nameless thing; nor did Caesar, who shared the agony, know for certain that he was killing the Republic as he went. Only Cicero, alternately reviling the Dictator and fawning upon him, somehow vaguely understood the torment inside Caesar. "For we are slaves to him," Cicero writes, "he himself to the times. So neither he knows what the times are going to demand of him, nor can we know what thoughts lie in his mind."

* * *

Caesar and his lieutenants, in their books on the Civil Wars, carry on the tale from the crossing of the Rubicon almost to the very end—and the military story is so spectacular that, with its blaze of martial brilliance, it hides the somber, yet more dreadful, story of the end of Rome as a Republic of free men.

Imagination can scarcely hold the dimensions of Caesar's activity in the five years that followed. The entire Mediterranean was the theater of action: distances of thousands of miles covered by racing foot-soldiers; stormy seas crossed in jerry-built fleets, hastily assembled; legions of Rome fighting Roman legions, defiling the eagles in Gaul and Spain, in Italy and the Balkans, in Greece, Egypt, Africa.

The narrative is paced, almost breathlessly, by the dash of Caesar's drive. He was across the Rubicon with the Thirteenth Legion on January 11. Rimini fell the next day, with other legions already racing down from Gaul to join the swoop. Six days later Pompey evacuated the capital—with him fled the Senate and the consuls. Swerving from his original target, Rome, Caesar dashed after them to south and east down the Adriatic coast to cut off their retreat. By February 19 he had reduced their first major resistance at Corfinium; behind him, Antony, in command of other legions now arriving from Gaul, mopped up the towns of northern Italy, as, one by one, their names a drumbeat of doom, they surrendered their garrisons or welcomed Caesar's standard-bearers. In less than two months Caesar had besieged Pompey at the southern tip of Italy, in the port of Brundisium; and, parley proving useless, Pompey fled across the Adriatic with the Roman fleet and his entourage. Turning back on Rome, Caesar entered the capital on April 1—to find no government to seize.

Back and forth now, across the map of the ancient world, Caesar flailed—first to Marseilles; then to Spain, to wipe out Pompey's Spanish legions in 49; then back across the Adriatic (in the spring of 48 B.C.) to challenge the new Republican armies which Pompey had gathered in Illyria. Bewildering his ponderous and aging rival with his speed and tactics, Caesar finally, with no more than a corps of troops (22,000 men) lured Pompey (with 47,000 men) to fight in the hills of Thessaly and, at Pharsalus, wiped out Pompey's forces in a day of slaughter. After which, more pursuit—for Pompey had escaped to the Eastern Seas; and not until late fall, arriving at Alexandria, did Caesar hear the news of Pompey's death.

Caesar records the fact starkly. But Plutarch and Dio, from sources still available to them (probably Pollio's history), tell it with more color. The severed head of his mighty rival was brought before him, as well as Pompey's signet ring, by the killers, who expected reward . . . and Caesar, seeing them, wept and lamented.

Well he might have wept. With Pompey's death, the chase was now to be endless, for Caesar was seeking more than victory, seeking something he could not wrench by arms—legitimacy, the mantle of the law. Somehow Pompey, in fleeing Rome with senators and consuls, in scattering them in flight about the Roman sea after his defeat, had shattered forever what Caesar sought to cement together.

Whether Caesar realized this immediately on arrival in Alexandria when he learned that now there was no leader left to bargain with or conciliate, or whether the tragedy only slowly seeped in on him, we do not know. He lingered long enough in Egypt, in the winter sun of

48/47 B.C., for all kinds of "ifs" and speculation:

Was it here, beneath the Pyramids, already ancient, or in the shadow of the desert temples that he began to think himself a God? The last authentic work which we have from Caesar's hand ends with his occupation of Alexandria (the later books of his Civil Wars are written by his scribes, staff or companions). Already it is different from the tart and spare Latin of his Gallic *Commentaries*. The Caesar of the Gallic *Commentaries* is an old-fashioned Roman brought up to believe that "*dulce et decorum est pro patria mori*," and his story of the Gallic war is told to thrill the citizens at home, to make them share his pride in Roman triumphs that shook the sky. The style changes in his Civil War volumes.[1] The soldiers now are "Caesar's soldiers," his personal legionaries. The style is more emotional, political, self-conscious— as when he is trapped in Spain, his troops surly after constant years of war, unpaid, resentful. Caesar thus cynically, writes of how he raised the money to pay them: "At this point, I borrowed money from the centurions

---

[1] Caesar was a master-stylist, and consciously so. The Caesar of the Gallic *Commentaries* is a delight to the ear, so simple in his phrasing that the book seems like bald battle-reporting. Yet it was not. A fragment of his discourses on rhetoric, quoted by later Roman stylists, has him saying: "*tamquam scopulum sic fugias inauditum atque insolens verbum*" (*Flee the little-heard and extravagant expression as you would a hidden reef*). It was thus he became the curse of schoolboys. His Latin in the Gallic *Commentaries* is so simple that teachers think it best for youngsters to start with Caesar before going on to the Greek elegance of Cicero. Yet where Cicero tasseled his involuted phrases about political banalities or commonplace gossip, Caesar's naked Latin was stripped only to make clear the greatest subtleties of war and politics, the behavior of men in combat, panic, courage and construction. Caesar's language is, indeed, simple; but the thoughts that rib the sentences are fit only for adult minds. In Rome, later, schoolboys were *rarely* taught Caesar's texts. Romans began their schoolboys in rhetoric with Cicero and Virgil.

and officers to pay the soldiers, thus at one stroke getting two results: binding the centurions to me by hope of repayment, and the soldiers by purchasing their goodwill with my largess." It is, however, at the close of his last volume that one hears most clearly the new voice of the changing Caesar: He records all the supernatural signs and portents that swept the world after his victory at Pharsalus—trumpetings and yellings had been heard as far away as Antioch in Syria; mysterious drums rolled in the temple of Pergamum; at Elis the statue of Victory revolved on its pedestal to turn away from the Goddess Minerva and face the temple doors in the direction of Pharsalus; and other omens. It is as if the Eastern Gods are welcoming and bowing to a new comrade in Heaven. The passage could not possibly have been written by the Republican Caesar who conquered Gaul; it is the voice of *Divus Julius*, the God Julius.

The winter stay in Egypt engages one of history's more interesting speculations, threading Caesar's stay there, through the Jews, to Christianity. As the Egyptians laid siege to him, Caesar with his handful of troops found himself cut off by the Mediterranean from quick reinforcement. The Jews of Palestine were among those who marched to his relief and he was grateful for this. Later, on returning to Rome, trying to re-create order, Caesar abolished all communities, separatist groups, collegia, workingmen's associations; but, in gratitude, he left the Jewish community untouched to manage its own affairs, a part of, yet apart from, the general community. A few generations later this Jewish community in Rome became the host of the infectious message of a Jew of Nazareth and his Jewish disciples who preached, within the Imperial Order, the doctrine of universal mercy.

From this community, protected by Caesar's original generosity, spread the infection of Christianity which, moving along the sensitive nervous system of the Roman establishment, made mercy as well as order one of the twin pillars of Western civilization.

For romantics, of course, the most alluring speculation is Caesar and Cleopatra. She was a goddess. She was also indisputably attractive, regal, queenly (later she even snubbed Cicero, a difficult thing to do). Of their sunset affair we know but little; yet it is reasonable, from Caesar's later hospitality to her, to assume that they twined about each other's bodies, however briefly. Whether it was a casual, political, or passionate affair we cannot judge. Yet the adulation of a bright and beautiful young woman is for men of middle age an intoxication—and, at this point, she was twenty-one and he fifty-four. If she was accepted as Goddess-Queen, certainly he was greater. There may or may not have been a baby boy as residue of their affair; learned scholars argue Cleopatra's pregnancy and dispute the evidence of Caesar's dalliance with her, either in the palace or on the famous spring voyage up the Nile. The unborn child could not, however it was, have been as great an influence on him as the perfumed, incense-laden atmosphere of an Oriental court where all kings were seen as Gods and no king reached the threshold of Caesar's wisdom.

In any event, he could not stay to see the child, if his, be born. He had to leave, Cleopatra's charms notwithstanding; for the world called. Nothing had been settled by the defeat and dispersal of Pompey's forces, or Pompey's death. All across the Mediterranean, resistance forces were mobilizing in the name of the Republic;

little Asian princelings plucked and bled the frontiers; in Rome itself, violence and commotion. There was so much work he had to do.

For it was all unfinished, and remained unfinished until the day he died. The thread of law and legitimacy that Pompey had snapped by fleeing Rome, carrying Senate and consuls with him, could not be raveled up again; and for the last few years of Caesar's stupendous exertions, we can see him only as pursuing that magic of legitimacy, the key to Republican power, which was forever to elude him.

From Egypt he circled the Mediterranean, mopping up pockets of resistance on his way back to Italy, then pushed directly on to Africa in one of the most hazardous of his gambles (one of the two for which Napoleon the Great, a devoted student of Caesar's campaigns, later criticized him).

In Africa the Republican forces had gathered ten Roman and four Numidian legions for their counterblow. Sailing unexpectedly across the winter-tossed sea, Caesar landed in Tunisia in early 46 with only 120 horse and 3,000 legionaries. As his beachhead was reinforced with more troops, he swiftly moved on his divided and quarreling enemies until in April 46, at Thapsus, he crushed them. Yet here again, the prize escaped him. Far more important than the Republican legions was their symbolic leader, Cato the Virtuous. Hating Caesar from the very beginning of his career, Cato even now, surrounded and doomed at Utica, would not yield. Spurning the forgiveness which Caesar offered if only Cato would return to Rome as senator and give his name to the process of new law, Cato preferred death—and at night, in his quarters, after reading Plato's *Phaedo*, Cato ran himself through with his sword. Thus, for Caesar it was on the march again, his wars incomplete, his title papers to power forever flawed.

There remained one final gathering of hostile Republican force, mobilized in Spain under the generalship of their last remaining military leader of size—Labienus.

It is difficult to fathom Labienus at this long remove in time. He is seen only fitfully in the years after his desertion at the Rubicon—occasionally in a Ciceronian reference, but usually through Caesar's plain and bitter relating of fact. Caesar's references to his old partner-in-arms are emotional to a degree found nowhere else in his writings; over the last years of life, Labienus was always there—for Caesar, an unhealed wound. There—leading the attack for Pompey against Caesar at Durazzo in 48; there—when, after a minor Pompeian victory in Illyria, Labienus captures some of the Gallic veterans and, as Caesar records, induces Pompey to give them to him and "apparently for the sake of display or to increase his own credit as a traitor brought them all out and, styling them 'comrades,' killed them in the sight of all"; there—goading Pompey to rashness, telling Pompey that Caesar's soldiers are no longer the veteran legions he himself helped shape in Gaul. Labienus stood with Pompey at Pharsalus, and Caesar makes a point of detailing Labienus' foolhardy tactical blundering. Escaping from Pharsalus, Labienus survived to fight Caesar again and to be defeated in Africa at Ruspina; survived again to flee to Spain and offer battle at Munda in April of 45, where Caesar finally caught up with him. Caesar had conquered —and Labienus died. The civil wars were at an end.

*   *   *

Labienus had deserted—thus, no mercy. The special rage that Caesar harbored for those closest to him when they betrayed his cause puckers through the composure of his writings again and again. One can sense the terror which he held for those who came too close.[2] Yet more important, by far, was his policy of mercy and forgiveness which baffled his enemies. A primitive of his age and culture, Caesar nonetheless had a proto-modern sense of statecraft; and wisdom, as well as inclination, made clemency a key to policy.

His mercies to opponents, conquered and beaten, have no match in the stories of ancient or modern tyrants. He had caught and captured the scheming Lucius Domitius Ahenobarbus (who so much wanted to replace him in command of Gaul) within a month of crossing the Rubicon. He released and forgave Domitius at Corfinium, sending all his baggage and personal treasures back with him—whereupon Domitius joined Pompey again, to oppose Caesar a few months later, commanding the defenses of Marseilles. Again at Marseilles, Caesar captured and released Domitius on parole. The third time he overtook

[2] Even his own beloved veterans, who had nothing left to believe in but Caesar, could taste this wrath. On one occasion, when his veteran Ninth Legion, tired of unending civil war, craving demobilization and their land, mutinied, Caesar called the cowards to muster and decimated 120 of their ringleaders. It is worth noting that decimation in the Roman sense was a much more terrifying, yet more reasonable, punishment than modern usage of the word implies. To decimate was to put to death, at random, one in ten of a group to be punished. In a cowardly cohort, it meant marshaling the men in a giant ring and ordering them to circle in the field single file. Then, at random, the punishing officer would choose one in ten of those who circled in file; the tenth man after that was also tapped; then the twentieth; then the thirtieth; and so on at intervals of ten. These men, so chosen by "decimation," or the counting off of ten, were those executed.

Domitius, however, at Pharsalus, his cavalry put Domitius to death.

To all Pompeian officers defeated in his first campaign in Spain (in 49) he offered honorable release, or promotion in his ranks; to all captured soldiers he offered immediate discharge, free passage home, or enlistment in his own legions. To both Afranius and Petreius, Pompey's commanding generals of the first Spanish campaign, he offered freedom-on-parole despite their previous barbarities to his own soldiers when captured. Afranius took up arms again, and when Caesar caught him a second time, Afranius died. Petreius was also defeated fighting Caesar a second time at Thapsus—and, knowing he had run short on Caesar's forgiveness, committed suicide. When Cato refused Caesar's mercy, Caesar granted the same mercy and their inheritance intact to Cato's wife and children; he did likewise for the family of Faustus Sulla, son of the dictator. His mercies—seen by moderns as practical politics—stretched back into the past: the descendants of all proscribed by Sulla, the Dictator, were restored to full citizenship; as were the descendants of those proscribed by Sulla's rival, Cinna. He refused to restore to full citizenship only those of Sulla's adherents who had murdered for pay.

Clemency was the cornerstone of his domestic politics. Refusing even to read the private correspondence of Pompey after his victory, he had the papers burned with all the names they contained; and restored Pompey's statue in his great theater. Enemies saw his clemency as vile, scheming, treacherous—"*insidiosa clementia*," Cicero called it privately. But Caesar was proud of the policy. To Cicero he wrote, "I am not moved when it is said of me that those whom I let go have departed to wage war

on me again, for there is nothing I like better than that
I should be true to myself and they to themselves." And
when, shortly later, Cicero also departed to join Pompey
and make war on Caesar, Caesar's grandness was unruffled. Thus, when in the fall of 47 B.C. Cicero (now
a helpless figure of humiliated fame) trudged on foot to
meet Caesar's landing at Tarentum and plead for mercy,
Caesar descended from his litter and walked on foot
many stadia back toward Cicero's refuge at Brundisium,
escorting the fallen consul through the dust to do him
honor. The names of others he forgave are too many to
list—but it is worth recalling that of the twenty conspirators known by name among the senators who joined in
assassinating him, no less than *ten* were Pompeian loyal-
ists whom he had pardoned after the civil wars.

Yet mercy earned him little of what he wanted. He
was a warrior with an all-conquering army—who wanted
not so much to conquer as to govern. To govern he
needed the only men Rome had trained for the task.
Thus he forgave them in order to use them—but they
could not live within his imagination, for their tradition
saw a world to be governed by the noble families of
Rome alone, a world for loot and enslavement, their
proper share of which Caesar would deny them. They
were the hereditary administrative corps who conducted
great affairs of state, wrote the treaties, collected taxes,
built roads, interpreted the Gods, governed provinces.
When he crossed the Rubicon, he ruptured the only
tradition Rome knew; and there was nothing left of the
Republic except memories and myths, meaningless phrases
come down from sturdy grandfathers, which to the nobles made their privileges and wealth seem like ancient
rights, and to the people made liberty synonymous with

anarchy and mob rule. No mercy could wean them from
their distortion of their own past.

Withdrawal and return, as historians have noted, is a
pattern common in the lives of great men—as if tempo-
rary absence from, and then return to, the scene of action gives men a clearer perspective, a larger, simpler
view of action when they come back. True of Mo-
hammed and Henry of Anjou, of Franklin Roosevelt,
Winston Churchill, Charles de Gaulle and John F. Ken-
nedy, it was true of Caesar also.

Of the last twenty years of his life, Caesar spent
little more than five years in Rome—adding up all his
visits and stays by day and month as best one can. In
the last five years of the Civil War he spent no more
than thirty days in Rome in 49 B.C., was away all of 48,
all of 47 except for two months. He was home in summer and fall of 46 for five or six months; and home again
for his longest stay in fifteen years—from October 45
to his death in March 44 B.C.

Each time that he paused in Rome, those last five
years, he must have become increasingly aware that
Rome would not work without his presence. It lacked
something—a sense of government. In his absence, the
mobs looted, killed and burned. Those whom he appointed or caused to be named consuls, tribunes, praetors
under his permanent dictatorship could not control the
street violence, or, worse, were so carried away by the
screaming and cheering of the mobs that they believed
that, actually, they *were* in control. Antony, Dolabella,
Caelius, even Trebonius took their appointments as
licenses to graft and snatch, enrich themselves and
avenge their grievances. For them, it was part of the

loot that was their due for following Caesar. Slowly, too, the political intelligence corps which Balbus had headed for Caesar when he was away in Gaul changed nature. Caesar's informers were now not merely intelligence agents of one among several politicians; they became the "*delatores*," the infamous secret police, of the governing Dictator, a menace to all who murmured in dissent; and, by the time of the reign of Tiberius, the scourge of innocent and guilty alike.

Thus, isolated from people and the traditional governing class alike by his own unbelievable eminence, a lonesome and solitary tyrant, surrounded by sycophants, fawners, slaves, and kissing-kneelers, Caesar sensed the increasing resentment of his rule. He knew how much old Rome resented the pressure and crowding at his court. Once after Cicero sat waiting overlong expecting to see him, Caesar remarked: "Can I have any doubt about how people loathe me, when even Marcus Cicero must sit waiting, and I cannot see him conveniently at a time that suits him? He is as pliable a man as is; yet I have no doubt he hates me."

This lonesomeness sets off the final prodigies of Caesar's career—for the accomplishments of his last brief stays in Rome are, even in modern terms, an unbelievable intellectual exertion. From his mind alone came a sequence of laws and decrees, in such frantic spasms of brief pauses between campaigns as to limn out the true Caesar—more philosopher than soldier. In their stark outlines—for we lack adequate detail—his statecraft sets out most clearly what Caesar was all about: a sense of order.

As High Priest and Dictator, he changed the calendar. Arbitrarily, he imposed Egyptian astronomy on the moon

calendar of the Romans, and, forever after, men's years
have been set by the revolution of the unimpeachable
sun, never again by priests, bankers or politicians manip-
ulating weeks and months for their own purposes. In 46
he spun out the laggard year to stretch for 445 full days!
Thereafter the year began on January 1 and closed on
December 31, as we know it today; and his Julian calendar was so accurate it persisted down to the eighteenth
century for all English-speaking peoples—and in Russia
until 1918, so that the first of the great twentieth-century
revolutions was still dated by Caesar's calendar.[3]

His reforms spanned all activity, and many of them
seem anachronistically pre-modern. He wrestled with
the problems of the cities, as we do today, and laid down
new laws to deal with their problems. A lover of beauty
and of gardens, of ivy, statuary and greenery, he willed
to the city of Rome all his private gardens and walks as
public parks. The swollen welfare rolls of Rome engaged
his attention—and he cut the relief rolls from 320,000 to
150,000 citizens entitled to free grain. He tackled credit
and restored some commercial stability to the system
ravaged by his own wars; put through tax reforms;
wrestled with the problems of labor and wages; and began to examine what we today call the problems of urban
environment. Rome was short of water, as all great cities
increasingly are, and no new aqueduct had been built
for her swollen population since 125 B.C.; he went to
work on the water problem; he rebuilt the harbor at
Ostia, Rome's main port; and tried to establish a system

[3] Caesar, it should be noted, was an amateur dabbler in the lore of
heaven and stars. Among his lost works, supposedly, is one, *De Astris*,
or *A Treatise on the Stars*, which indicates that in those long and lonesome nights at camp and in battle he must have turned his thoughts to
astronomy also.

of public libraries.[4] He curbed the street gangs and began
to empty Rome of its drifting mobs by giving them free
land in the Empire, where they were settled as colonists
with fields of their own to work.

Many of Caesar's efforts seem so familiar today that
even his failures make us wince. He tried to reorganize
the crowded city traffic that choked the streets of Rome
and, of course, like all men dealing with urban traffic ever
since, failed. He failed, too, in his sumptuary laws—a late
effort to restrict ostentation, luxuries, fornication and divorce and impose an antique and outworn morality by
fiat. To those of his contemporaries who still remembered
his youth and lancemanship, the strictures of the Dictator
must have seemed the ultimate hypocrisy.

His greatest failure, however, was where he tried his
hardest—for, perhaps, he himself did not understand
what he had done. Caesar tried to re-create the Republic.
Rome was now to be, in Caesar's mind, a city in the service of its empire, the *res publica* to be worldwide. Thus,
he arbitrarily increased the Senate's membership from
600 to 900, packing it with rough centurions and field
legates, men of merit risen from the ranks, as well as

---

[4] It was Pollio, our narrator of the action at the Rubicon, who
finally built the first public library which Ceasar never lived to see.
Pollio, after the crossing of the Rubicon, was called to war; as a
general he achieved decisive successes; as a politician he was even
more successful. Alone among those who surrounded Caesar at the
Rubicon, he lived to die a natural death through all the proscriptions
and murders that followed. When, late in life, in Augustus' reign, he
retired, he was already rich with the booty of his conquests, and his
homes and gardens were famous. He wrote, of course, his famous
history of the civil wars which has disappeared except in the quota-
tions and fragments that other Roman historians took from it. In his
wealth and old age, he was a patron of poets, writers, artists, vicari-
ously living the literary life which, in his youth, he had hoped for.
And it was Pollio who opened the first library in Rome where all citizens might freely have access to books for the first time.

breech-bound Gauls and strange Spaniards. (Balbus not only became a senator himself, and later consul, but Balbus' home town of Gades—now Cádiz—in Spain was fully enfranchised as a Roman colony.) Second-class citizens were now to be enfranchised—Sicilians, Alpine Italians, Gauls, Jews.

As a crowning gesture, Caesar planned to build a Saepta such as Rome had never dreamed of. The Saepta was where the Romans gathered to vote their laws and choose among their candidates. The old Saepta in the Campus Martius was an open enclosure where citizens assembled on call of magistrates, waited for the auspices, then filed through their lanes to cast ballots in a basket, much as Western voters do today. It was nicknamed the "*ovile*," or sheepfold, because the voters marching through their lanes so much resembled sheep. When it rained, they soaked; in the climactic election, for consulate, which by the old calendar fell in Fifth Month, now called July, they must have sweltered in the Italian sun. Caesar proposed to do the voters honor—by building a marble temple, a mile in circumference, where they might sit to hear the speeches, roofed from rain and storm, and where the sacred act of voting might take place. Even Cicero thrilled at the plan.

It was fitting that Caesar did not live to see the completion of his temple to the voting process—for the voting process had lost its meaning as soon as Caesar crossed the Rubicon. He now, himself, controlled the voting process by flat of sword. On one occasion in a supreme gesture of contempt, on the very last day of December, an incumbent consul having died, he assembled the voters to elect his friend Caninius, one of his old lieutenants of the Gallic war, to fill out the unexpired term—which lasted until sundown of the day, and the end of the year. But forever after Caninius was a "consular," having earned his honor by whimsy of the dictator as a second-string football player earns his letter in the last minute of the big game by whimsy of the coach. The marble Saepta, beautiful but hollow of meaning, was finished some time after Caesar's death by Augustus' favorite, Agrippa; and the outcropping of its ruins may be seen today. It is better to think of the last Saepta as an Augustan, rather than a Caesarian, monument; Augustus was a cynic; he had no illusions.

In Caesar, more clearly than in any other historic character, ancient or modern, one sees the terrible conflict between the idea of liberty and the idea of order. Rarely does any civilization harness the two; but when that happens the results can be as spectacular and magnificent as they were in Republican Rome; in ancient Athens; in England at its apogee; in the United States for how long we do not know.

Caesar was enamored of liberty—the idea, and his reverence for it, throbs through all his early writing. Constantly, as he writes of the Gauls in his Gallic *Commentaries*, he gives them all credit for their love of liberty —balanced with contempt for their inability to govern themselves. When he must put Dumnorix, the Gallic chieftain, to death for breaking parole, he records the chase of Dumnorix and tells how, even as Dumnorix was being hacked to death, "he constantly shouted that he was a free man, and the citizen of a free country."

Liberty was in Caesar's blood as it was in the blood of all high-born Romans. Caesar could see that it was liberty for the few, not the many; yet the many could not administer their liberties once they sought power in the streets.

The idea of free men governing themselves rests on a common morality, on a common responsibility shared. When all citizens share roughly the same standards, the idea works. But when people identify their animal appetites and narrow greeds with rights and justice, the whole concept of self-government collapses; and those who call them to account, when they are wrong, are lumped as tyrants along with men of evil who earn that title by their cruelties.

It is difficult to condemn "the people" when they are wrong—for to repudiate by name what claims to be the people's will has been, in every time and every culture, the ultimate sacrilege. However misguided, wicked, bestial or immoral the mobs that masquerade as people may become, to denounce them is heresy. It was heresy in the words of Isaiah and Christ; it was heresy in Confucian China even as it is today in Communist China—the "people" are always right. It is heresy in Russia, in the popular democracies, in America—and it was heresy in ancient Rome, too.

Thus, Caesar was required by his times to be a heretic —not a heretic in Cato's terms, which saw heresy as repudiation of the Gods and Roman tradition, but a heretic in his own terms, as a *popularis*, as one who came to power presenting himself as an expression of the people's will. Yet he learned that the people of his time could not govern; and that they needed government more than they needed liberty—despite what the mobs, or the poets, or the senators claimed the people's will to be.

Paranoia is the occupational disease of leaders—the greater their power, the greater their danger. In this century, as the tools of technology and communication concentrate power as dangerously as Roman development concentrated it in the Forum, we have known many paranoiacs—Stalin, Hitler, Mao Tse-tung and a dozen lesser madmen. Even in civilized countries like France, where leaders are not entirely separated by their own power from information and reality, the disease of paranoia threatens leadership. A man set apart from others and endowed with power is trapped by his triumph in a cage of his own making.

So it was with Caesar. The last authentic glimpse we have of Caesar shows the distance and awe that surrounded him in his last days. Fittingly, it comes through the eyes of Cicero in a letter written on December 19, 45 B.C., three months before the assassination. Caesar is now a solitary who travels with a bodyguard of two thousand men. No friends are left him, only servants. He carries with him all the burden of empire wherever he goes—and alone. Slaves and couriers speed after him to alert him to the news. Three months later, on news of the assassination, Cicero, who writes this letter, is to somersault with glee at the killing of the man who had forgiven him. But now, in December, Cicero is flattered beyond containment by the fact that Great Caesar, the Dictator, should visit him for the Saturnalian holidays at his estate in Puteoli, overlooking the blue bay of Naples. Cicero is annoyed, of course, by the fact that Caesar visits him not as a counselor of state, one ex-consul visiting another ex-consul, but as a man of letters visiting another author. But let Cicero give us the last glimpse as he writes to his friend and publisher Atticus:

"What a fearsome guest! And yet I do not regret his visit, for it was so pleasant. On the second day of the

Saturnalia he put up for the night at the villa of Philippus [Augustus' stepfather], but his troops so packed the house that there was hardly a room left for Caesar to dine in—two thousand men he had with him. I was naturally worried about what would happen next day, but Cassius Barba came to my rescue. He posted guards, who made camp in the fields and protected my villa.

"Caesar stayed with Philippus until one o'clock of the next day. Nobody was admitted to his presence; he was going over the budget, I believe, with Balbus. Then [coming here], he took a walk on the seashore and at two o'clock a bath. Then word was brought to him that Mamurra[5] [was dead]—[he took it] without the slightest change of expression in his face.

"He took an oil rub-down before sitting to dinner. Since he was going through an emetic purge, he ate and drank without fear, quite jolly. It was a fine dinner, if I say so myself, well seasoned and cooked—and the conversation matched the food.

"In three other rooms Caesar's staff was lavishly entertained. His freedmen and slaves of lower rank had all they could eat, and the upper ranks ate elegantly. What more shall I say?—I showed off as a good host.

"As for my guest—he is not one to whom you would say, 'I'd love to have you stop off on your way back to

---

[5] Mamurra was Caesar's chief engineer in the Gallic campaign. He must have been very close to Caesar, and probably quite loathsome, for both Cicero and the poet Catullus (above all, Catullus) find Caesar's association with Mamurra unbearably contemptible. How evil a man Mamurra may have been we cannot guess; the extravagant denunciation of Catullus makes it seem, however, that Mamurra, more than anyone else, was connected with the dark side of Caesar's nature. Whatever Caesar felt about Mamurra and his death, it is doubtful that he would have shown his emotions in the presence of Cicero, a great gossip and one who despised Mamurra.

stay with me.' Once is enough.

"The talk avoided anything serious—mostly we dis-
cussed writing. In short, he was both pleased and delight-
ful. He was to spend one day in Puteoli, the next at Baiae.

"There you have the story of his visit—or should I
say his encampment? As he [left], passing Dolabella's
villa, the whole armed bodyguard formed up in files, to
right and left of him. . . ."

Three months later he was dead—bodyguard of two
thousand men notwithstanding.

We must reconstruct those last three months of Caesar's life from distant and partisan sources, for the assassination was a curtain drawn between two worlds, and
has haunted writers ever since as do all great assassina-
tions.

What has come down to us comes at far remove in
time—except for Cicero's letters of the weeks of dread,
and an account by a Greek courtier, Nicolaus of Damascus, who includes an almost clinical report of the killing
in his story of Augustus. The clinical interest in the body
—even to the debate as to whether it was twenty-three
or thirty-five punctures in the corpse—strikes a modern
echo. Most of what we know, however, comes from the
telling of Plutarch and Suetonius, writing more than a
century after the event, with access to what sources we
do not know.

In such accounts we dimly see Caesar several times
again in the weeks that followed Cicero's last glimpse of
the Dictator. And each time that we see him, he is strange
—psychopathically distant and arrogant. It was only a
fortnight after visiting Cicero that, on December 31,
he so casually assembled the voters with such contempt

to name Caninius as consul for half a day. We have several reports of his appearances in the first few weeks of January—dressed now in an all-purple toga, like an Eastern king, crowned with a laurel wreath in public, sitting on a gilded chair when he appears on the rostra. Upon him, now, the Senate heaps slavish honor upon honor; a temple of Clementia celebrating his mercy has been erected in his honor; his statues rise in the city. He himself is so busy that he does not conceal his contempt for the men who now sit on the Senate benches. On one occasion, as he sits in the Forum, supervising the clearing and rebuilding of the central place of the dirty, overcrowded city, a delegation of senators headed by a consul marches out to report to him the latest resolutions of honor. Caesar, preoccupied in inspecting the construction, dealing with artisans and contractors, does not even rise to greet them, continues his conversations, then, after finishing his papers, still seated, casually and negligently lets them pay their respects to him.

We see him twice in February—once when he accepts from the Senate the title of *Dictator Perpetuus*, and again, the same week, at the Festival of Lupercal on February 15. It was at the Lupercal festival, of course, that Mark Antony offered him the crown of king, as he sat on his golden seat above the rostra. Though accounts of the episode differ with the political prejudices of later authors, all agree that he did refuse it, feigningly or not. Shakespeare probably had it right when he imagines Antony as saying, "You all did see that on the Lupercal I thrice presented him a kingly crown, which he did thrice refuse." For Caesar was, by now, more than king. He was the man who shaped the world and made its weather. Nicolaus of Damascus records, "He began to think of himself as superhuman, and the common people worshipped him; but he began to be obnoxious to the nobles and those who sought a share in government."

His assassination followed the Lupercal episode by only a month.

One must see as backdrop to his assassination Caesar's last great enterprise—for he meant to venture deep into Asia. While he had been in Gaul, conquering the West, his old crony Crassus had tried to conquer the East and been destroyed (in 53 B.C.) with his legions by the Parthians. So long as the Parthians from Asia menaced the West, the world was in disorder—and thus they, like Gaul and Germany, must be brought to submission. On March 18, 44 B.C., Caesar was to set forth again with the legions to subdue the Parthians—Asia was the last great challenge to his world order.

Nothing solid about these plans may be gotten from the writings of the ancients—only the echo of millennia-old gossip. Was Caesar so driven by madness and a sense of his own divinity as to believe that Asia, too, could be brought under Western rule? Or was he unwilling to let another, younger general command the legions, perhaps to return in five or ten years from Gaul to challenge him as he had challenged Pompey? Or was he simply so tired of politics, intrigue, gossip ("I have lived long enough," he said, "to satisfy both nature and glory") and the climate of his court as to seek out once again the clean, astringent atmosphere of battle where all men fall in order by their rank, and duty is clear, though bloody?

Rome must have buzzed as he prepared to leave. Would he take Cleopatra with him? (She had come from Egypt to dwell those last few months in one of Caesar's villas by the Tiber.) If so, as ancient gossip has it, was he so swayed by her as to be leaving Rome not just for war but to make a new capital, an imperial capital, somewhere in the East?

At Alexandria, with Cleopatra?

He was scheduled to march out at trumpet blast, leading his legions with their eagles, on March 18. For March 15, the Ides of March, he had, therefore, summoned the Senate to a last meeting before departure—presumably to hear his nominations, promotions, laws, decrees and last injunctions.

For those who hated him, now, if ever, was the chance to strike—before he was once more encased and armored in iron legions. So they prepared. It is difficult to fit together the fragments of report that we still have. From what comes down to us, this is how it happened:

The Senate was to meet in early morning. The auspices were unfavorable. He would not come. They sent delegations to plead with him to come. Later—shortly before noon—he decided after all to come. Sources differ —some say he walked, others that he was borne in his litter. The plot was quite clever. Mark Antony, his burly loyalist and swordsman, would be detained in conversation just outside the meeting place—a hall off the portico of Pompey's theater—by an old companion of the Gallic wars, Trebonius, now among the plotters. If Antony or others gave trouble, hired killers were available—some sixty to eighty gladiators nearby in the pay of the conspiracy. Caesar, who came late, upset their timetable further by talking, privately and at quite some length, with Popilius Leanas. Then he ascended his curule chair. All conspirators had daggers, hidden in those little writing boxes the senators normally used to hold their styli and wax tablets for notetaking.

Tullius Cimber moved first—he approached Caesar, pleading for forgiveness for his brother, a Pompeian in exile. Cimber fell groveling at the Dictator's feet and tugged at the hem of his robe, thus pinning Ceasar in place.

This was the signal.

Servilius Casca, behind Caesar, struck first, stabbing him in the left shoulder, a glancing blow a little above the collarbone. Caesar, cursing, struck back with his pointed stylus. Cassius Longinus slashed at his face. Casca called to his brother, who stabbed Caesar in the side. Then the other conspirators, all round, struck—among them Marcus Brutus, who lanced him in the groin. To Marcus Brutus, nephew of Cato, son of one of Caesar's old mistresses, Caesar had shown special mercy, even forgiving him for fighting with Pompey at Pharsalus. A Greek historian reports that Caesar called out, "You, too, Brutus my son"—but, although scholars question the fancy, the ancient Greek phrase, with a variation of reading, might be translated as "Brutus, you son of a bitch." Then all fell on him, stabbing and sticking him as if he were a boar to be slaughtered, for all had sworn that they would share the bloodshed. Thus he died, sinking at the foot of Pompey's statue, re-erected by his grace, while the conspirators, smeared with blood, gazed, then fled. The physician Antistius, who made the final examination of the cadaver, counted twenty-three wounds—only one of which, he thought, was thoroughly fatal; in other words, a bungling butcher's job.

Caesar's body was carried off after some hours; troops were brought into the city; and the Dictator's remains were burned on the site of what later became the Temple of Julius, whose ruins one may still see a few hundred feet from the rostra and the Senate in the Forum—in the shadow of the Capitoline, where Jupiter's Temple stood. The night of the cremation the mobs rioted again, taking flame all across the city, putting torch to the homes of as many of the conspirators as they could identify.

After that, all, assassins and Caesarians alike, accepted him as *Divus Julius*, the God Julius Caesar, who would live forever.

Those who killed Caesar thought that if the single man were erased, the Republic would automatically flourish, liberty with it, and all good citizens rally to their cause. But those who rallied were few. On the very night of the assassination, March 15, Cicero (who was not in on the plot), hearing the news, rushed to pen a note to one of the assassins: "I congratulate you, I rejoice, I love you, I shall guard you. . . . What's happening, what's going on . . . ?" Yet, within three weeks the verdict of history was in, and Cicero, too, knew that the assassination had solved none of those problems of liberty and order that had vexed Rome for a century. "If Caesar," wrote Cicero on April 7, quoting a friend, "with all his genius could not find a way out, who will do so now?"

The Republic was dead. Not for eighteen hundred years would there be another great attempt at self-government by free men until the Americans tried it.

A BIBLIOGRAPHY OF
JULIUS CAESAR

A complete bibliography of Caesar would take almost as many pages as this book; thus this bibliography limits itself to a few works found in English, or English translation. In no sense comprehensive, it offers only a few of those books which have teased my imagination, and which may satisfy an appetite on the part of the reader to fashion his own Caesar.

LILY ROSS TAYLOR: *Party Politics in the Age of Caesar.* Berkeley: University of California Press, 1961.

LILY ROSS TAYLOR: *Roman Voting Assemblies.* Ann Arbor: University of Michigan Press, 1966. (Professor Taylor, an adornment to our scholarship, is, by all odds, the greatest living American student of Caesar. Her knowledge of ancient politics is infused with the keenest interest and understanding of contemporary politics.)

J. P. V. D. BALSDON: *Julius Caesar: A Political Biography.* New York: Atheneum, 1967. (This is the most readable one-volume study of Caesar's career published in English in recent times.)

MATTHIAS GELZER: *Caesar: Politician and Statesman.* Oxford: Blackwell's, 1968. (Galley proofs of this work were generously lent me by Sir Basil Blackwell. It is the most scholarly, best documented, and most detailed study of Caesar done in modern times. Accepted by all scholars as the masterwork by the great German authority, it is hard going for the average reader, but worth the effort.)

E. G. SIHLER: *The Annals of Caesar: A Critical Biography*. New York: G. E. Stechert & Co., 1911. (This work —alas, now out of print—dates from the beginning of serious American scholarship in the classics. Commonly held in contempt by most modern scholars, Sihler's refreshing naïveté, free-wheeling style, and enormous industry make his book still a pleasure to read.)

JOHN DICKINSON: *Death of a Republic*. New York: Macmillan, 1963. (A very conservative view of Caesar as a dangerous radical.)

REX WARNER: *The Young Caesar*. Boston: Little, Brown–Atlantic Monthly Press, 1958.

REX WARNER: *Imperial Caesar*. Boston: Little, Brown–Atlantic Monthly Press, 1960.

For young readers:

JOHN GUNTHER: *Julius Caesar*. New York: Random House, Landmark Books, 1959.

For general background:

THEODOR MOMMSEN: *The History of Rome*. New York: Meridian Books, 1958 (paperback). (Mommsen still towers over all other scholars of Rome. For detail, sweep, eloquence, and sheer literary magnitude, he is matchless. His original works are out of print in English. But this paperback abridgment is first class.)

MASON HAMMOND: *City-State and World State*. Cambridge: Harvard University Press, 1951.

FRANK BURR MARSH: *The Founding of the Roman Empire*. Austin: University of Texas Press, 1922.

F. R. COWELL: *Cicero and the Roman Republic*. New York: Chanticleer Press, 1948.

H. H. SCULLARD: *From the Gracchi to Nero*. London: Methuen, University Paperbacks. New York: Barnes & Noble, 1958.

SIR RONALD SYME: *The Roman Revolution*. New York: Oxford University Press, 1939. Paperback edition, 1960.

For two views of Caesar in English translation by a Frenchman and an Italian:

GUGLIELMO FERRERO: *The Life of Caesar*. New York: W. W. Norton, 1962.

GERARD WALTER: *Caesar*. London: Cassell, 1953.

Of the ancient authors and sources, the most important contemporary works are:

JULIUS CAESAR: *The Gallic Wars*.

JULIUS CAESAR: *The Civil Wars*.

MARCUS TULLIUS CICERO: *Letters to Atticus*.

MARCUS TULLIUS CICERO: *Letters to His Friends*.

MARCUS TULLIUS CICERO: *Orations and Essays*.

CATULLUS: *Poems*.

SALLUST: *Bellum Catilinae and Other Writings*. (All of the above are to be found in the Loeb Classical Library, published by Harvard University Press. The reader should be warned that many of these translations are very poor—bald, stumbling, frequently inaccurate. But they are the standard in the field.)

The best translation of Caesar himself I have found to be:

REX WARNER: *The War Commentaries of Caesar.* New York: New American Library, Mentor Books, 1960.

Other ancient authors who can still delight (in addition to the enormous corpus of Cicero), all of whom may be found in English translation:

Plutarch's Lives.

DIO: *History.*

SUETONIUS: *Life of Caesar* (included in his *Twelve Caesars*).

NICOLAUS OF DAMASCUS: *The Education of Augustus.*

VELLEIUS PATERCULUS: *Roman History.*

Three fantasies of superlative literary quality that may enlarge the reader's imagination:

THORNTON WILDER: *The Ides of March.* New York: Harper, 1948.

ROBERT GRAVES: *I, Claudius.* New York: Smith and Haas, 1934. Now available in the Modern Library.

ROBERT GRAVES: *Claudius the God.* New York: Smith and Haas, 1935. Paperback edition: Vintage Books. (Both of these works by Graves fall in a much later period than Caesar's. But the author's imagination gives a remarkable portrait of the imperial city.)

Two other books that have particularly intrigued me:

KEITH G. IRWIN: *The 365 Days: The Story of Our Calendar.* London: Harrap, 1965.

JOHN WESLEY HEATON: *Mob Violence in the Late Roman Republic.* Urbana: University of Illinois Press, 1939.

THEODORE H. WHITE

Born in Boston, Massachusetts, in 1915, Theodore H. White attended Boston Latin School and was graduated summa cum laude from Harvard University in 1938. That year he received the Frederick Sheldon Traveling Fellowship and got as far as China, where he became correspondent of *Time* magazine in 1939. He was later named chief of the China Bureau of *Time* and served in that capacity until 1945. At the end of World War II he returned to the United States, and in 1946 his first book (written with Annalee Jacoby), *Thunder out of China*, was published. After serving for a brief time as editor of *The New Republic*, he edited the *Stilwell Papers*. In 1948 he went to live in Europe, where he served for a while as European correspondent for *The Reporter*, and completed his second book, *Fire in the Ashes*, published in 1953, the year he returned to the United States. The following year he was national correspondent for *The Reporter* and in 1955 became national correspondent for *Collier's* magazine. His first novel, *The Mountain Road*, was published in 1958, and his second, *The View from the Fortieth Floor*, in 1960. In 1961, Theodore H. White published *The Making of the President—1960* and for it he won the 1962 Pulitzer Prize. *The Making of the President —1964* followed in 1965. For his writing of the television documentary *The Making of the President—1960*, Mr. White received an Emmy Award as well as television's Program of the Year Award. He also wrote the television documentaries *The Making of the President—1964*, and *China: The Roots of Madness*, for which he won another Emmy. Mr. White lives in New York City with his wife and two children.

DATE DUE
